VIOLIN EDITIO

BOOK ONE

MW01028471

Orchestra Expressions

Lead Author: **Kathleen DeBerry Brungard**
Authors: **Michael L. Alexander**   **Gerald E. Anderson**   **Sandra Dackow**
Contributing Editor: **Anne C. Witt**
Contributing Arrangers: **Jack Bullock, Victor Lopez, Tom Roed**

Art Credits

Bullfighting Scene: passing the cape. Pablo Picasso (1881–1973) © 2003 Estate of Pablo Picasso/Artists Rights Society (ARS), New York. Transparency: © Réunion des Musées Nationaux/Art Resource, NY. Student page: 9

Flower and Barbed Wire at Berlin. Michael Pole © Michael Pole/CORBIS. Student page: 18

Untitled 1989 (red and yellow figures on stand). Keith Haring. © The Estate of Keith Haring. Student page: 24

Conversation, 1992. Bridget Riley. Oil on linen. © 2002 Bridget Riley, All Rights Reserved, Courtesy Karsten Schubert, London. Transparency: Reproduced by courtesy of Abbot Hall Art Gallery, Kendal, UK. Student page: 30

Study for a Tapestry (study for Spatial Ikat III), 1976. Lia Cook (b. 1943). Serigraph on paper, 9 1/4 x 15 11/16 in. (23.4 x 39.9 cm.). © Lia Cook. Transparency: © Smithsonian American Art Museum, Washington, DC/Art Resource, NY. Student page: 38

Stalking Panther (Prowling Panther). 1891–1892. Bronze.by Phimister Proctor (1862–1950). © 2003. Reprinted courtesy of Phoenix Art Museum, Arizona/Western Art Associates/Bridgeman Art Library. Student page: 45

Mochibana (Rice Cake and Flowers) by Keiko Kodai. 17 x 12 1/2 in. © 2002 The Wing Gallery. Student page: 49

United States Naval Academy Graduation Hat-Toss Photograph Courtesy of the United States Naval Academy Photography Lab, Annapolis, Maryland. Student page: 52

Expressions Music Curriculum™, Music Expressions™, Band Expressions™, Jazz Expressions™,
Orchestra Expressions™, and Guitar Expressions™
are trademarks of Alfred Publishing Co., Inc. All Rights Reserved.

4 5 6 7 8 9 10   10 09 08 07
© 2004 ALFRED PUBLISHING CO., INC.
All Rights Reserved

LEFT HAND SHAPING

Warm-ups

Perfect Posture!

- Move from a seated position to a standing position and back.

- Adjust your posture and balance so your feet do not move when moving from sitting or standing.

- Sit on the front part of the chair.

Waves

- Extend your arms in front of you with palms down.

- Move your arms in parallel motion upward and downward, side to side, and in circles.

- Repeat motions with palms up.

- Repeat the same two exercises with your arms moving in opposite directions.

Finger Sit-ups

- Raise your right hand to eye level with your palm facing you.

- Keeping your fingers curved, squeeze your right forearm with your left fingertips (left thumbnail facing you).

- Leave all fingers down while you raise and tap each individual finger (begin with your fourth finger).

Finger Flex

- Extend your arms in front of you.

- Make a fist in both hands.

- Gently flex your fingers out as far as you can.

- Repeat several times.

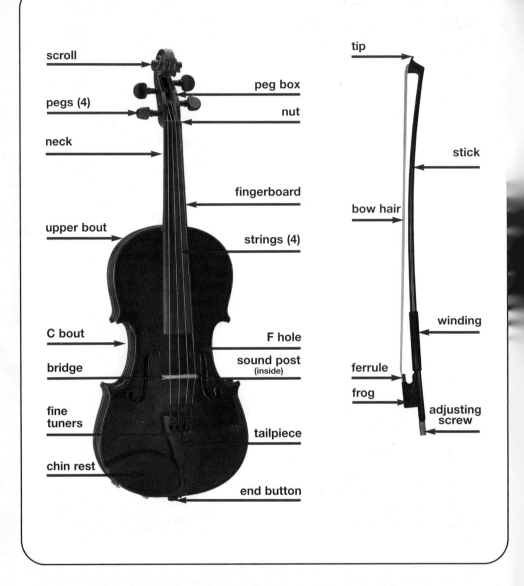

Care of the Instrument

- Wash your hands before handling the instrument.

- Be careful when handling the instrument. It is fragile and can be damaged or broken if dropped, bumped, or struck against other objects.

- Keep a clean, soft cloth in the case to wipe fingerprints and rosin dust from the strings, instrument, and bow stick after playing.

- Do not turn the pegs until taught to do so by your teacher. Strings and other parts can be easily broken.

- Never allow others to play the instrument.

- When you are not using the instrument, store it in its latched case.

- Store the instrument in a place of moderate temperature. Never leave it in a very hot or cold automobile.

- Do not attempt to repair the instrument. Consult your teacher.

- Always remove the shoulder pad before placing the instrument in the case.

- Never hang the instrument from a music stand.

Rest Positions

- Stand and place the instrument in rest position under your right elbow.

- Place your left hand on the upper bout of the instrument under the neck.

- Face the bridge out, away from your body.

- Sit near the front of the chair with your feet flat on the floor.

Violin Rest Position—
Standing

Violin Rest Position—
Seated

Violin Rest Position—
Seated

Care of the Bow

- Do not touch the hair of the bow against your fingers, face, hair, or other surfaces.

- Be careful when handling the bow. It is fragile and can break if struck, dropped, or bumped.

- Remove the bow and place it on the music stand before unpacking the instrument.

- Before playing, tighten the bow hair with the adjusting screw. Your teacher will demonstrate the correct tension.

- After playing, loosen the bow hair with the adjusting screw. Your teacher will demonstrate how much to loosen the bow.

- Place the bow in the case after packing the instrument.

Note to Parent/Guardian: Important for your child's musical development are the following accessories:

- Soft Cloth
- Violin Rosin
- Violin Shoulder Pad
- Folding Music Stand

- Metronome
- Pencil(s)
- Extra set of strings

RIGHT HAND SHAPING
Warm-ups   CD 1:3

Penny Push-ups

- While seated, balance a penny on the back of each hand with fingers pointed forward.

- Slowly move up and down, side to side (knee to knee), in opposite directions, and in straight lines from your left shoulder to your right knee.

- Let your wrists bend.

Dueling Hands

- With both hands, palms facing down, wave slowly and smoothly. Then wave quickly and choppily.

- Next, wave your left hand slowly and smoothly, and at the same time, wave your right hand quickly and choppily.

- Finally, wave your right hand slowly and smoothly, and at the same time, wave your left hand quickly and choppily.

Ping-Pong

- While seated, hold a small ball in your right hand with your palm facing down (a ping-pong ball works best).

- Slowly bend your wrist upward and downward and side to side, and then wave at the teacher.

- Keeping your knuckles facing forward, trace a straight line from your left shoulder to your right knee.

- Keeping your palm facing down, trace a straight line from knee to knee.

- Let your wrists bend.

LEFT HAND SHAPING

Warm-ups CD 1:3

Orchestra Stretch #1

- Place your right hand over your left shoulder.

- With your left palm on your right elbow, gently push your right hand farther over your left shoulder.

- Reverse arms and repeat.

Orchestra Stretch #2

- Reach as high as you can and make a fist with both hands.

- Gently flex your wrists upward and downward and then side to side.

- Gently flex your fingers in and out.

Playing Position

- Move to standing rest position.

- With your left foot, take a slight step forward to 11 o'clock and balance your body on the balls of your feet (the area just behind your toes).

- Place your right hand on the bottom of the instrument with your thumb underneath the button.

- Your left hand should be on the upper bout of the instrument, under the neck.

- Lift the instrument above your head and swing it over slightly to the left.

- Rest the instrument on your left shoulder.

- Set your jaw line in the chin rest.

- The end button should point to the middle of your neck where your collarbones meet.

- Your arm should form a straight line from your knuckles to your elbow.

Over Head

Above Shoulder to the Side

Front View

Back View

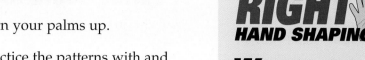

Finger Pattern Drill

- This exercise is for both hands or just the left hand if using both is too difficult.

- Relax your arms and hold them straight out in front of you at eye level.

- Turn your palms up.

- Practice the patterns with and without music.

1 2 3 4 Open Pattern

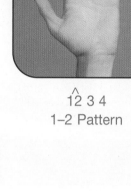

1 2̂3 4
2–3 Pattern

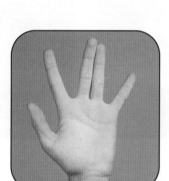

1̂2 3 4
1–2 Pattern

1 2 3̂4
3–4 Pattern

1 x 2 3 4
Bass Pattern

RIGHT HAND SHAPING

Warm-ups CD 1:3

Knee Benders

- Holding the instrument in standing playing position and your feet in playing stance, bend at the knees and move upward and downward.

Sidewinder

- In seated playing position, turn from your waist slightly from side to side.

Creative Tools of Music

Improvisation—the spontaneous creation of music within specific guidelines

Creative Expression—Improvise Rhythm Patterns on the Open A String

Orchestra @ Home

LESSON 1

1. Demonstrate to your family how to unpack and pack the instrument.
2. Identify the parts of the instrument and bow we learned today.
3. Practice warm-ups with Masterwork #1: "Les Toréadors" From *Carmen* by Georges Bizet (*zhorzh bee-**zay***) (CD 1:3).
4. Demonstrate rest position to your family.
5. Pluck the A string to the steady beat of "Les Toréadors" (CD 1:3).

LESSON 2

1. Practice warm-ups to CD 1:3, "Les Toréadors."
2. Review the parts of the instrument and bow you have circled in your book.
3. Discuss the care of the instrument and bow with your family.
4. Demonstrate both rest and playing position with Perfect Posture!
5. In rest position, play the open A string to the steady beat of CD 1:3.

LESSON 3

1. Practice warm-ups and stretches to CD 1:3.
2. Practice Finger Pattern Drill to CD 1:3, keeping a steady beat. Change the pattern every eight beats.
3. Practice moving from rest position to playing position.
4. Practice the playing position warm-ups on page 4.
5. In rest position, play the open A string with a steady beat to CD 1:3, "Les Toréadors."

LEFT HAND SHAPING

Warm-ups

Perfect Posture!
Orchestra Stretches #1 and #2
Finger Pattern Drill

Finger Pattern Sit-ups

- Raise your right hand to eye level.

- Place your left hand around your right arm in the 2-3 finger pattern.

- Leave your other fingers down while you raise and tap each individual finger.

Finger Twister Games

- With both hands, palms facing up, tap the tips of your thumbs and your fingers together in the following patterns.

Finger Twister Game #1

Left Hand   1 2 3 4 – 1 2 3 4 repeat
Right Hand 1 2 3 4 – 1 2 3 4 repeat

Finger Twister Game #2

Left Hand   1 2 3 4 – 1 2 3 4 repeat
Right Hand 2 3 4 1 – 2 3 4 1 repeat

Finger Twister Game #3

Left Hand   4 3 2 1 – 4 3 2 1 repeat
Right Hand 3 2 1 4 – 3 2 1 4 repeat

Finger Twister Game #4

Left Hand   3 4 1 2 – 3 4 1 2 repeat
Right Hand 1 2 3 4 – 1 2 3 4 repeat

Left Hand Strumming

- Keeping your thumb in place, strum the strings with your left hand by reaching across all four strings with the fourth finger.

Left Hand Pizzicato

- Keeping your thumb in place, pluck the individual A, D, and G strings with the fourth finger of your left hand.

Creative Tools of Music

Pizzicato (pizz.)—pluck the string

Pizzicato Position

As you look down the instrument, from left to right, the strings are:

G   D   A   E
low   high

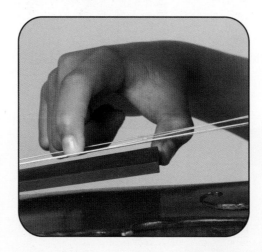

Left Hand Playing Position

- Form the shape of a "C" in your left hand with the fingers lightly curved.

- Cradle either side of the neck in the "C," supporting it between the pad of your thumb and the base knuckle of your first finger.

- Check to see if there is space in the "valley" between your thumb and first finger by inserting a pencil with your right hand.

- The left wrist joint should be straight and the elbow tucked under the center of the instrument. Point your left elbow toward your belt buckle.

Bow Hold on Pencil

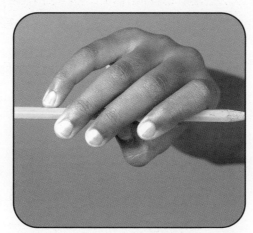

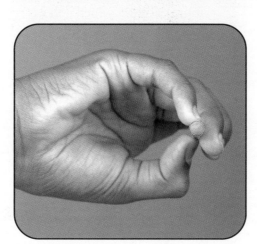

- Hold out your right hand, palm up, with fingers curving inward in a relaxed manner.

- Touch the end of your thumbnail to the outer joint of your second finger, not the tip of the finger.

- Place the pencil between the thumb and second finger.

- Turn your pencil so it lies between the middle and outer joint of the first finger and on the tip of the fourth finger.

- Make sure your thumb is bent outward!

 Creative Expression— Improvise Rhythm Patterns on the Open A, D, and G Strings

Orchestra @ Home

LESSON 1

1. Practice warm-ups and stretches to CD 1:3, "Les Toréadors."

2. Practice proper pizzicato technique. Pluck the open strings to the steady beat of CD 1:13–16.

3. Demonstrate to your family Left Hand Strumming and Left Hand Pizzicato in playing position. Practice keeping a steady beat with CD 1:3.

LESSON 2

1. Review warm-ups to CD 1:3. Concentrate on making clean, clear finger changes in the Finger Twister games.

2. Practice Left Hand Strumming and Left Hand Pizzicato.

3. Draw a line from the middle joint of the first finger to the tip of the fourth finger. Practice placing the pencil along this line as you set your bow hold.

4. Practice Bow Taps, Thumb Flex, and Body Taps with a pencil.

LESSON 3

1. Perform warm-ups with CD 1:3.

2. Perform left hand warm-ups.

3. Play pizzicato to a steady beat using all four strings. Use CD 1:13–16 for accompaniment.

4. Demonstrate to your family the bow hold on a pencil.

5. Perform right hand warm-ups to the music of CD 1:3.

RIGHT HAND SHAPING

Warm-ups
CD 1:3

Penny Push-ups
Dueling Hands
Ping-Pong
Knee Benders
Sidewinder

Bow Taps

- Hold a pencil vertically in your right hand.

- Tap one finger at a time in rhythm to the music.

- Begin with your fourth finger. Do not tap your thumb.

- Keep your fingers and thumb relaxed and curved.

Thumb Flex

- Hold a pencil vertically in your right hand.

- Flex your thumb in and out.

- Keep your fingers and thumb relaxed and curved.

- Finish with the thumb flexed outward.

Body Taps

- Hold a pencil vertically with the point upward.

- Touch the eraser to the top of your head, your left shoulder, your right knee and then your left knee.

- Keep your fingers and thumb relaxed and curved.

- Repeat.

Bow Motion Game

- Using the pencil bow hold, touch your bow thumb to your left shoulder.

- Now touch your bow thumb to your right knee (thigh if standing), following a straight line.

- Repeat.

7

UNIT 3

 LEFT HAND SHAPING

Warm-ups CD 1:3

Perfect Posture!
Orchestra Stretches #1 and #2
Finger Pattern Drill
Finger Pattern Sit-ups
Finger Twister Games #1, #2, and #3
Left Hand Strumming
Left Hand Pizzicato

Creative Tools of Music

ABA Form—a musical form consisting of three sections in which the third section is the same as the first: same, different, same

Bar Line—the vertical line that divides the music staff into measures

Clef Sign—a symbol placed at the beginning of the staff used to identify the lines and spaces.

March—rhythmic music for the uniform movement of groups of people

Measure—the space between two bar lines to form a grouping of beats

Music Staff—five lines and four spaces on which notes and other musical symbols are placed

Opera—a play set to music in which most of the dialog is sung

Plot—a brief description of the story

Quarter Note—a note one quarter the length of a whole note; in this book, a quarter note equals one beat

Quarter Rest—a rest one quarter the length of a whole rest; in this book, a quarter rest equals one beat

Repeat Sign—the symbol with two lines and two dots that means to perform a section or a composition again

Time Signature—a symbol at the beginning of the staff indicating how many beats are in each measure and what kind of note gets one beat

Timeline—shows a span of history with specific events placed when they occurred

8

Bullfighting Scene: passing the cape.
Pablo Picasso (1881–1973)

Carmen

This story takes place around 1820 in Seville, Spain. Carmen is a beautiful young woman who works in a factory. She flirts with many men, including a young Army officer and a bullfighter. "Les Toréadors" announces the exciting entrance of the bullfighters as they parade to the bullring. Even though the Army officer desperately loves her, Carmen flirts with the dashing bullfighter. As a tragic result, Carmen is killed by the jealous Army officer as she is about to attend the bullfight.

©2003 Estate of Pablo Picasso/Artists Rights Society (ARS), New York.
Transparency: ©Réunion de Musées Nationaux/Art Resource, NY.

RIGHT HAND SHAPING

Warm-ups

CD 1:3

Dueling Hands
Knee Benders
Sidewinder
Bow Taps
Thumb Flex
Body Taps
Bow Motion Game

PORTRAIT

Georges Bizet

Georges Bizet was a French composer who lived from 1838 to 1875. As a composer he was most noted for his operas. In his opera *Carmen*, he incorporates the rich nationalistic tradition of Spanish folk music, song, and dance. Even though *Carmen* was unsuccessful at first, it has become the world's most popular opera.

19th-Century Romantic Style

Carmen is a good example of the 19th-Century Romantic characteristics of strong emotion, nationalism, and lush writing for orchestra.

Timeline

BAROQUE 1600–1750	CLASSICAL 1750–1820	ROMANTIC 1820–1910	MODERN/CONTEMPORARY 1910–PRESENT

1600	1700	1800	1900	2000

End of American Civil War 1865

Carmen 1875

Alexander Graham Bell invents the telephone 1876

"Les Toréadors" Listening Map

A section	**B** section	**A** section
|: A :| contrasting material | A	B B¹	A

Descriptors: _____ _____

 ## Creative Expression—Improvise Movement to ABA Form

Orchestra @ Home

LESSON 1

1. Perform the warm-ups to CD1:3, "Les Toréadors."

2. Review the names and definitions of the Creative Tools of Music (vocabulary) you learned today.

3. Clap/count/sing/play pizzicato lines 4–6 with CD 1, Tracks 4–6.

4. Tell your family the plot of the opera *Carmen*.

LESSON 2

1. Perform the warm-ups CD 1:3.

2. Clap/count/sing/play lines 4–7 with CD 1:4–7, keeping a steady beat. At our next lesson, you will demonstrate playing these lines to the steady beat of the CD accompaniment.

3. Tell your family about the composer Georges Bizet (zhorzh bee-**zay**) and the 19th-century Romantic style.

LESSON 3

1. Perform the left hand and right hand warm-ups to CD 1:3.

2. Play lines 4–7 pizzicato with their CD tracks. Remember to observe the repeat signs.

3. Explain to your family the "Les Toréadors" Listening Map. Play CD 1:3, for them and identify the **ABA** sections.

4. Play for your family your own "Les Toréadors" (line 7) pizzicato with its CD track.

UNIT 4

 **LEFT HAND SHAPING**

Warm-ups CD 1:8

Perfect Posture!
Orchestra Stretches #1 and #2
Finger Twister Games #1, #2, and #3
Left Hand Strumming
Left Hand Pizzicato

Creative Tools of Music

Arco—play with the bow

◼ Down Bow—pull the bow toward the tip

Hoo-hoo—a cardboard tube/PVC pipe used to shadow bow

Ledger Lines—short lines to extend the range of the staff higher or lower

Shadow Bow—bow without a sound on the arm or lap

∨ Up Bow—pull the bow toward the frog

9 Vivaldi on G CD 1:9

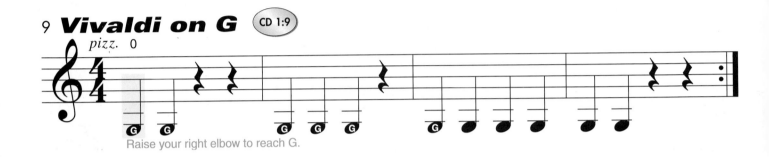

Raise your right elbow to reach G.

10 Two String Reggae CD 1:10

11 Three Point Shot CD 1:11

Say the note names as you play.

12 Mix 'em Up CD 1:12

Say the note names as you play.

 Creative Expression—Draw Creative Tools of Music (Worksheet #4)

10

Bow Hold on Bow

RIGHT
HAND SHAPING
Warm-ups   CD 1:8

Dueling Hands
Knee Benders
Sidewinder
Bow Taps
Thumb Flex
Body Taps
Bow Motion Game

(Perform each rhythm line eight times.)

• Make sure your thumb contacts the stick between the winding and the frog.

13 *Rhythm No. 1*   CD 1:13
Say the bowings as you play.

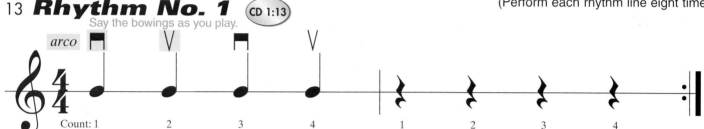

14 *Rhythm No. 2*   CD 1:14
Relax your bow hold.

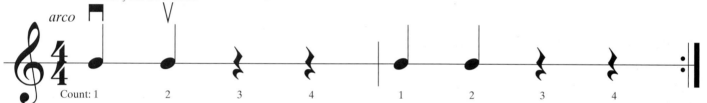

15 *Rhythm No. 3*   CD 1:15
Use your elbow and wrist joints.

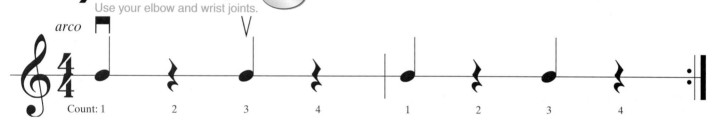

16 *Rhythm No. 4*   CD 1:16
Pull a straight bow!

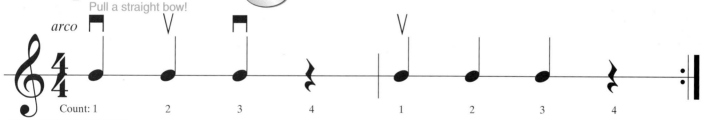

Orchestra @ Home

LESSON 1

1. Perform warm-ups to CD 1:8, "Ode to Joy" from *Symphony No. 9* by Ludwig van Beethoven (pronounced **lood**-vig fahn **bay**-toe-ven).

2. Clap/count/sing/play lines 9–10 pizzicato with their CD tracks.

3. Practice placing the bow hold on the bow. It is not necessary to tighten or loosen the bow.

LESSON 2

1. Perform warm-ups to CD 1:8.

2. Clap/count/sing/play lines 9–12 pizzicato with their CD tracks.

3. Carefully tighten the bow hair. Place the bow hold on the bow. At our next lesson, you will demonstrate your best bow hold.

4. Practice bowing lines 13–16 with a Hoo-Hoo. Carefully loosen the bow hair.

LESSON 3

1. Perform warm-ups to CD 1:8.

2. Sing and play lines 9–12 pizzicato with their CD tracks.

3. Practice placing the bow hold on the bow.

4. Shadow-bow lines 13–16 using a Hoo-Hoo with their CD tracks.

5. If necessary, complete the Creative Expression (Worksheet #4).

UNIT 5

LEFT HAND SHAPING

Warm-ups CD 1:8

Perfect Posture!
Orchestra Stretches #1 and #2
Finger Pattern Drill
Finger Pattern Sit-ups
Finger Twister Games
Left Hand Strumming
Left Hand Pizzicato

Creative Tools of Music

Intonation—how well each note is played in tune

Rosin—hardened tree sap applied to the hair of the bow to produce a sound

Finger Patterns on the D String

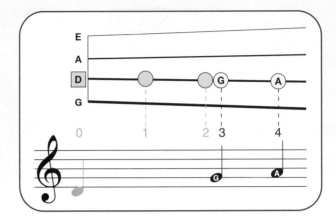

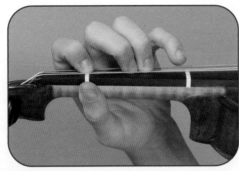

G = 3 Fingers Down   A = 4 Fingers Down

17 **New Way to Play A** CD 1:17
Press the string firmly to the fingerboard.

18 **New Note G** CD 1:18

19 **Pumping Iron #1** CD 1:19

Keep the left elbow tucked under the instrument.

20 **Pumping Iron #2** CD 1:20

HOW TO ROSIN THE BOW

- Hold the rosin firmly in the left hand.
- Using a proper bow hold, pull the bow across the rosin in smooth and even strokes, both down-bow and up-bow.
- Make sure the rosin is equally applied across the hair from the frog to the tip.

Bow Levels

A String   D String   G String

RIGHT
HAND SHAPING

Warm-ups CD 1:8

Knee Benders
Sidewinder
Bow Taps
Thumb Flex

---

21 *A String Level* CD 1:21

Relax your bow hold.

22 *D String Level* CD 1:22

Bow flexing your elbow and wrist joints.

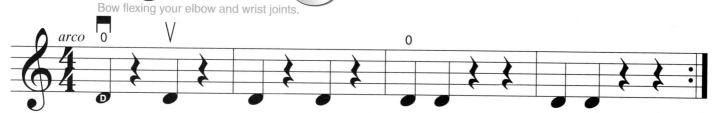

23 *G String Level* CD 1:23

Raise your right elbow to reach G.

 Creative Expression— Compose (Worksheet #5)

Orchestra @ Home

LESSON 1

1. Perform warm-ups to CD 1:8, "Ode to Joy."

2. Trim your fingernails to the proper length.

3. Play lines 17–20 with their CD tracks. Match your notes to the melodies in the CD.

4. Use a hoo-hoo to shadow bow lines 21–23 with their CD tracks.

5. Bring a soft cloth to orchestra class.

LESSON 2

1. Perform warm-ups to CD 1:8.

2. At our next lesson, you will demonstrate the proper left hand, finger, wrist, and arm position for the D string.

3. Play lines 17–20 pizzicato with their CD accompaniments. Match your notes to the string melody.

4. Demonstrate the bow levels, keeping your bow straight between the bridge and the fingerboard.

LESSON 3

1. Perform warm-ups to CD 1:8.

2. Play music lines 17–20 pizzicato with their CD tracks. Match the pitches of the melody as you play.

3. Play music lines 21–23 arco with their CD tracks. Keep your bow straight between the bridge and the fingerboard.

4. Complete your composition (Worksheet #5) and play it pizzicato and arco for your family.

Finger Patterns on the D String

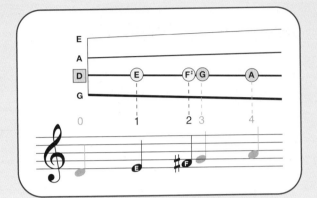

 ## LEFT
HAND SHAPING

Warm-ups   CD 1:8

Perfect Posture!
Orchestra Stretches #1 and #2

Creative Tools of Music

Double Bar—two vertical lines placed on the staff to indicate the end of a section or composition

♯ **Sharp**—a sign that raises a note one half step

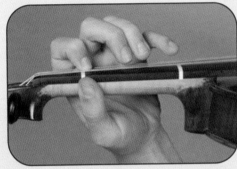

E = 1 Fingers Down

F♯ = 2 Fingers Down

24 New Note F♯   CD 1:24
Press the string firmly to the fingerboard.

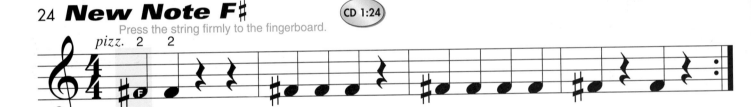

25 New Note E   CD 1:25

26 Shuffle Back and Forth   CD 1:26

27 Mary Lee*   CD 1:27

Folk Song, England
No repeat sign, keep going!

*Memorize the music that has an asterisk following the title.

RIGHT HAND SHAPING
Warm-ups CD 1:8

| Knee Benders | Bow Taps |
| Sidewinder | Thumb Flex |

 Creative Expression—Compose (Worksheet #6)

28 **Cross Bows** CD 1:28
Check your bow hold.

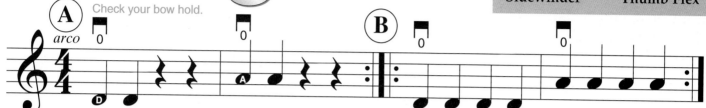

29 **Double Cross** CD 1:29

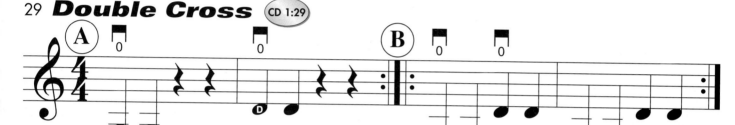

30 **Cross Roads** CD 1:30

31 **Border Crossing** CD 1:31

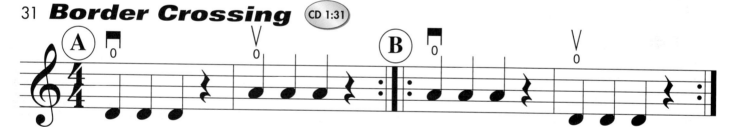

32 *Lacrosse* CD 1:32

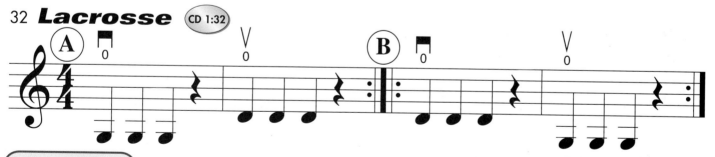

Orchestra @ Home

LESSON 1

1. Perform warm-ups to CD 1:8, "Ode to Joy."

2. Practice lines 24–25 pizzicato with their CD tracks. Match F# and E with the melody line notes of the CD accompaniments.

3. Practice lines 28–29 arco with their CD tracks. Practice the bow arm levels silently on the string before playing the lines.

4. Review lines 17–20 pizzicato with their CD tracks.

LESSON 2

1. Perform warm-ups to CD 1:8.

2. Practice lines 24–27 pizzicato with their CD tracks. Strive to play in tune.

3. Practice lines 28–32 arco with their CD tracks. Feel the change of your bow arm level.

4. Complete your four-measure composition. Perform your composition pizzicato for your family.

LESSON 3 & 4

1. Perform warm-ups to CD 1:8.

2. Practice lines 24–27 pizzicato with their CD tracks. Keep fingers curved and hovering over the string.

3. Practice your original composition pizzicato and play it for your family. You will perform your composition at the next class meeting.

4. Practice lines arco 28–32 with their CD tracks.

LEFT HAND SHAPING

Warm-ups CD 1:8

Perfect Posture!
Orchestra Stretches #1 and #2
Finger Pattern Sit-ups
Finger Twister Games

Fingerboard Sliding

- Place the instrument in playing position with the left hand set to play E on the D string.

- Rest all four fingers lightly on the string. Do not press into the string.

- Slide your entire hand so that your thumb comes to a rest in the crook of the neck.

- Lightly slide back to the E note position. Make sure all fingers slide on the string and that your thumb moves with your hand.

Fingerboard Tapping

- Place the instrument in playing position with the left hand set to play E on the D string.

- Tap your first finger four times on the string so you can hear a sound.

- Move your hand so your thumb comes to a rest in the crook of the neck.

- Tap your first finger four times here.

- Repeat with each finger.

33 Bass Shift CD 1:33

Check your left hand position.

34 Bass Hit CD 1:34

35 Safe at First CD 1:35

36 Good King Wenceslas* CD 1:36

Christmas Carol, Wales

Keep a steady beat.

Creative Expression—Improvise Using F♯, E and D

Creative Tools of Music

Bow Lift—raise the bow from the string and return it to the original starting point

Shift—move the left hand from one point on the fingerboard to another

Bow Lifts

- Set the bow hold on your pencil.
- Rest the pencil on your left shoulder and then draw a straight line to touch your right knee.
- Lift your arm in an arch to land on your shoulder again.
- Repeat the entire process.

RIGHT HAND SHAPING
Warm-ups   CD 1:8

Knee Benders
Sidewinder
Bow Taps
Thumb Flex

Orchestra @ Home

LESSON 1

1. Perform warm-ups to CD 1:8, "Ode to Joy."
2. Practice lines 33–35 pizzicato with their CD tracks. Keep all fingers curved over the fingerboard. Match the pitches of the string modeling in the CD accompaniment.
3. Practice lines 37–38 arco with their CD tracks. Practice each line slowly before playing with the CD accompaniments.

LESSON 2

1. Perform warm-ups to CD 1:8.
2. Practice lines 33–36 pizzicato with their CD tracks. Match your notes with the melody in the CD accompaniment.
3. Practice bow lift lines 37–39 arco with their CD tracks. Set the bow on the string after each lift.
4. Complete "Bows 'n' Notes" (Worksheet #9) and perform it for your family with its CD track. Practice it!

LESSON 3

1. Perform warm-ups to CD 1:8.
2. Practice lines 33–35 with their CD tracks.
3. Practice memorizing "Good King Wenceslas" by singing and playing it pizzicato.
4. Practice lines 37–39 arco with their CD tracks.
5. Perform "Bows 'n' Notes" with its CD accompaniment.

Warm-ups (CD 1:8)

Perfect Posture!
Orchestra Stretches #1 and #2
Fingerboard Sliding
Fingerboard Tapping
Knee Benders
Sidewinder
Bow Taps
Thumb Flex
Bow Lifts

Creative Tools of Music

Penta—a Greek word meaning "five"

Pentascale—an arrangement of five notes in ascending or descending order

Phrase—a complete musical thought; a building block of themes; a musical sentence

Scale—an arrangement of notes in ascending or descending order

Symphony—a large composition for orchestra usually made of four distinct movements

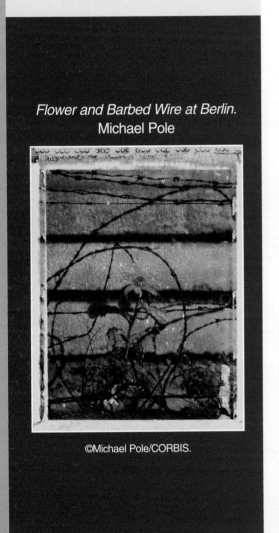

Flower and Barbed Wire at Berlin.
Michael Pole

©Michael Pole/CORBIS.

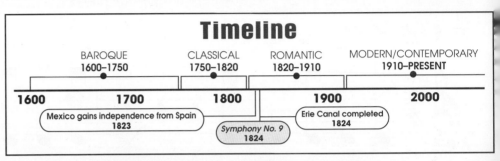

Timeline

	BAROQUE 1600–1750	CLASSICAL 1750–1820	ROMANTIC 1820–1910	MODERN/CONTEMPORARY 1910–PRESENT
1600	**1700**	**1800**	**1900**	**2000**

Mexico gains independence from Spain 1823

Symphony No. 9 1824

Erie Canal completed 1824

"Ode to Joy" Listening Map

Phrases in "Ode to Joy" Theme:	A	A¹	B	A¹	B	A¹
No. of measures in each phrase:	4	4	4	4	4	4

Thematic Descriptor: _____

PORTRAIT

Ludwig van Beethoven

Ludwig van Beethoven was a German composer who lived from 1770 to 1827. As a composer, he was most noted for his nine symphonies. Although he began to lose his hearing in his early thirties, a great deal of Beethoven's most outstanding works were written after he became totally deaf. Beethoven used the "Ode to Joy" in his ninth (and final) symphony to demonstrate his support for equality and the universal brotherhood of mankind.

41 High Top Sneakers (CD 1:41)

(A) Press the string firmly to the fingerboard.

42 Snow Shoes (CD 1:42)

43 Flip Flops (CD 1:43)

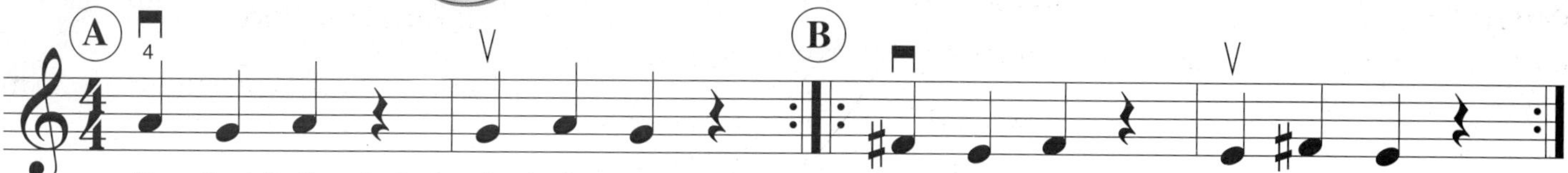

Keep the left elbow tucked under the instrument.

44 Au Claire de la Lune* (CD 1:44)

Relax your bow hold.

Folk Song, France

45 Slavonic Folk Song* (CD 1:45)

Bow flexing your elbow and wrist joints.

Folk Song, Eastern Europe

46 Pentascale #1 (CD 1:46)

47 Ode to Joy* (CD 1:47)

LUDWIG VAN BEETHOVEN, Germany

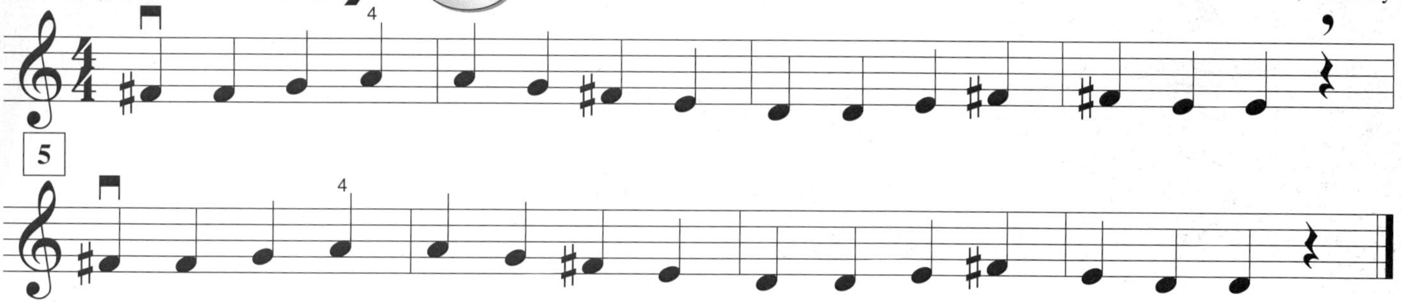

Creative Expression— Create Movement to "Ode to Joy"

Orchestra @ Home

LESSON 1

1. Perform warm-ups to CD 1:8, "Ode to Joy."
2. Practice lines 41–43 shadow-bowing and arco with their CD tracks. Practice the lines slowly at first until your bow and fingers match. Listen for the melody and match the pitches with your notes.
3. Tell your family the story of Beethoven and his *Symphony No. 9*.

LESSON 2

1. Perform warm-ups to CD 1:8.
2. Practice lines 41–46 pizzicato, shadow-bowing, and arco with their CD tracks.
3. At our next lesson, you will show your left and right hand coordination by playing "Au Claire de la Lune" and "Slavonic Folk Song."

LESSON 3

1. Perform warm-ups to CD 1:8.
2. Practice lines 44–47 with their CD tracks. Practice lines 44 and 45 from memory.
3. Explain the structure of "Ode to Joy" to your family.
4. Perform "Ode to Joy" pizzicato and arco for your family. Use its CD accompaniment.

UNIT 9

Warm-ups CD 1:48

Perfect Posture!
Orchestra Stretches #1 and #2
Finger Pattern Drill

Finger Pattern Sit-ups
Left Hand Strumming
Left Hand Pizzicato

Knee Benders
Sidewinder

Bow Taps
Thumb Flex

Finger Patterns on the A String

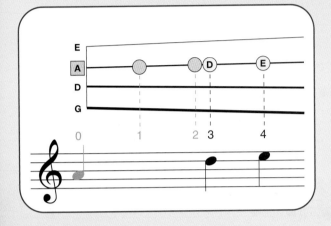

D = 3 Fingers Down

E = 4 Fingers Down

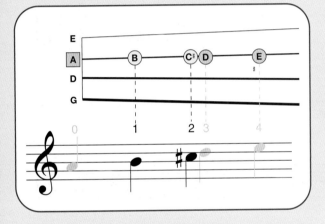

B = 1 Finger Down

C# = 2 Fingers Down

49 New Way to Play E CD 1:49

Press the string firmly to the fingerboard.

50 New Way to Play D CD 1:50

51 Pumping Iron #3 CD 1:51

Say "lift."

52 Pumping Iron #4 CD 1:52

53 **Play C♯** CD 1:53

Press the string firmly to the fingerboard.

54 **Play B** CD 1:54

55 **Back and Forth Shuffle** CD 1:55

56 **Hip Hop Jumps** CD 1:56

Keep all left hand fingers curved over the fingerboard.

Creative Expression—Compose (Worksheet #11)

Orchestra @ Home

LESSON 1

1. Perform warm-ups to CD 1:48, "Hoedown."

2. Use the pictures and descriptions on page 20 to prepare your fingers to play on the A string. Trim your fingernails to the proper length.

3. Play lines 49–52 pizzicato with their CD tracks. Match your pitches to the string model melodies.

4. Strive to play lines 44–47 from memory with a clear tone quality using their CD accompaniments.

LESSON 2

1. Perform warm-ups to CD 1:48.

2. Practice lines 53–56 pizzicato with their CD tracks.

3. Review lines 49–52 shadow-bowing and arco with their CD tracks. Match your notes to the melody in the CD accompaniment.

4. Practice all lines for performance at our next lesson.

5. Complete your composition (Worksheet #11) and the additional game.

LESSON 3

1. Perform warm-ups to CD 1:48.

2. Play lines 49–56 pizzicato, shadow-bowing, and arco with a clear tone quality using their CD tracks.

3. Show your family your composition and perform it for them. Use your favorite CD rhythm track (13–16) if you like. Prepare to perform it at the next class meeting.

LESSON 4

1. Perform warm-ups to CD 1:48.

2. Play lines 49–56 pizzicato, shadow-bowing, and arco with a clear tone quality using their CD tracks.

UNIT 10

Warm-ups (CD 1:48)

Perfect Posture!
Orchestra Stretches #1 and #2
Fingerboard Sliding
Fingerboard Tapping

Knee Benders
Sidewinder
Bow Taps
Thumb Flex
Bow Lifts

Creative Tools of Music

Arpeggio—notes of a chord played one at a time

Chord—three or more notes that sound at the same time

Subdivision—the inner pulse of the beat

57 Shifting Gears (CD 1:57)

58 Down Shift (CD 1:58)

Keep all left hand fingers curved over the fingerboard.

59 Speed Shift (CD 1:59)

60 Automatic Shift (CD 1:60)

61 Pentascale #2 and Arpeggio (CD 1:61)

62 Cruise Control* (CD 1:62)

Play with a full sound.

GERALD ANDERSON, U.S.A.

63 Tongawallah* CD 1:63

Folk Song, Hindustani

64 Dreidel* CD 1:64

Holiday Song, Hanukkah

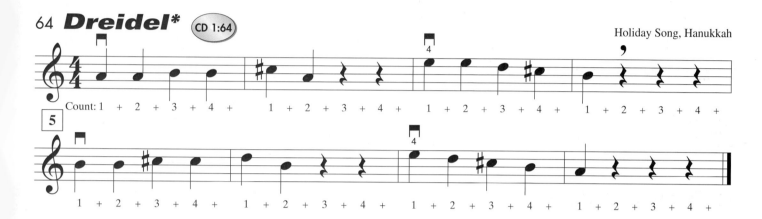

65 It's the Blues, Man!* CD 1:65

Keep a steady beat.

JACK BULLOCK, U.S.A.

Creative Expression—Improvise Using A, B, and C♯

Creative Expression—Compose (Worksheet #14)

Orchestra @ Home

LESSON 1

1. Perform warm-ups to CD 1:48, "Hoedown."

2. Review lines 49–50 and 53–54 pizzicato, shadow-bowing, and arco with their CD tracks.

3. Practice lines 57–61 pizzicato, shadow-bowing, and arco with their CD tracks.

4. Experiment with notes A, B, and C♯ in improvisation. For fun, use CD rhythm Tracks 13–16.

LESSON 2

1. Perform warm-ups to CD 1:48.

2. Practice lines 57–60 shadow-bowing and arco with their CD tracks.

3. Practice line 61 slowly and carefully. Watch for the repeat signs. You will perform this line from memory at our next lesson. Concentrate on intonation, tone, and string bass shifting.

4. Practice melody 62 shadow-bowing and arco, observing the bow lifts.

5. Practice melodies 63–64, counting the subdivision.

6. Prepare your composition (Worksheet #4) for performance.

LESSON 3

1. Perform warm-ups to CD 1:48.

2. Practice songs 63–65, counting the subdivision. Shadow-bow and arco each song.

3. Practice your composition and play it for your family. You will perform it for the class at our next lesson.

UNIT 11

Warm-ups CD 1:48

Perfect Posture!
Orchestra Stretches #1 and #2
Fingerboard Sliding
Fingerboard Tapping
Knee Benders
Sidewinder
Bow Taps
Thumb Flex
Bow Lifts

Creative Tools of Music

Balance Point of the Bow— the point where the stick remains totally horizontal when balanced on the forefinger

Ballet—a story told through music and dance

Bridge—a transitional musical passage connecting two themes or sections

Coda—a short ending section of music

Double Stop—two notes played at the same time

♪ **Eighth Note—**a note one half the value of a quarter note

Introduction—a short section of music at the beginning of a composition

Phrases—the different sections of a theme

Synopsis—a brief overview of the story

$\frac{2}{4}$ **Time Signature—**a symbol at the begining of the staff indicating how many beats are in each measure and what kind of note gets one beat

PORTRAIT

Aaron Copland

Aaron Copland was an American composer who lived from 1900 to 1990. As a composer, he was most noted for his ballet and film music. Many of his most famous works such as *Billy the Kid, Appalachian Spring,* and *Rodeo* take their themes from American folklore. *Rodeo* has become a very popular ballet, and the music is often performed on the concert stage. The nationalist style is reflected when a composer uses the folk melodies or patriotic songs of his country in his compositions. Folk melodies and songs may be found in work songs, lullabies, religious songs, and dance music of any particular country. Copland characterized American nationalism in *Rodeo* through his use of cowboy songs and fiddle tunes from the American West. Through his many compositions featuring American folk melodies, Copland is recognized as the most important American composer in the nationalist style.

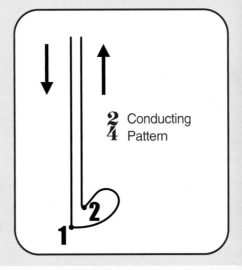

$\frac{2}{4}$ Conducting Pattern

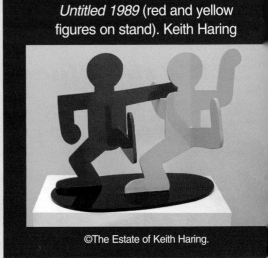

Untitled 1989 (red and yellow figures on stand). Keith Haring

©The Estate of Keith Haring.

Timeline

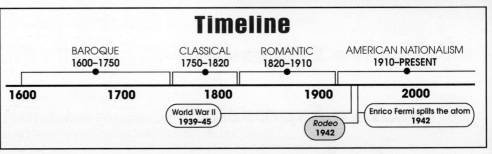

	BAROQUE 1600–1750	CLASSICAL 1750–1820	ROMANTIC 1820–1910	AMERICAN NATIONALISM 1910–PRESENT
1600	**1700**	**1800**	**1900**	**2000**

World War II 1939–45

Rodeo 1942

Enrico Fermi splits the atom 1942

"Hoedown" Listening Map

	Intro	**A** section	**B** section	music slows	**A** section	Coda
Music:	"tuning"	*Bonyparte*	*McCleod's Reel*	"the kiss"	*Bonyparte*	
Phrases:	Intro	ABABBAA	CDCE(E-ext.)	Intro material	ABBA(A-ext.)	closing

Descriptors: _____ _____

66 *California Surfboard* CD 1:66

Use a fast bow stroke for eighth notes.

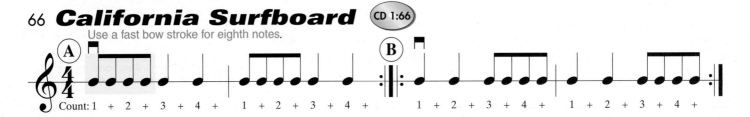

24

67 Bile 'em Cabbage Down* CD 1:67

Bow with your elbow and wrist joints.

Folk Song, U.S.A.

68 Dune Buggy CD 1:68

Count: 1 + 2 + 1 + 2 + 1 + 2 + 1 + 2 + 1 + 2 + 1 + 2 +

69 Pentascale #1 and Arpeggio Variation CD 1:69

70 Mountain Bike CD 1:70

Vary the bow speed for eighth and quarter notes.

71 Double Stops CD 1:71

Balance the bow on both strings.

72 Lowdown Hoedown* CD 1:72

Bow with your elbow and wrist joints.

SANDRA DACKOW, U.S.A.

2nd time: Yeehaw!

Creative Expression—Improvise Movement to "Hoedown"

Orchestra @ Home

LESSON 1

1. Perform warm-ups to CD 1:48, "Hoedown."

2. Tell your family about eighth notes and how they are counted.

3. Practice lines 66–67 shadow-bow and arco. Concentrate on bow division and bow speed.

4. Tell your family about the ballet *Rodeo*.

LESSON 2

1. Perform warm-ups to CD 1:48.

2. Practice lines 68–70 with their CD tracks. Vary the bow speeds for quarter and eighth notes. Prepare line 69 for performance, concentrating on bow speed and intonation.

3. Demonstrate for your family how to conduct "Hoedown" in 2/4.

LESSON 3

1. Perform warm-ups to CD 1:48.

2. Practice line 71 with its CD accompaniment. Be sure to keep equal weight on each string.

3. Explain how double-stops work and play line 72 for your family.

4. Explain the "Hoedown" Listening Map to your family as you listen to CD 1:48.

UNIT 12

Warm-ups CD 1:73

Perfect Posture!
Orchestra Stretches #1 and #2
Finger Pattern Drill

Finger Pattern Sit-ups
Left Hand Strumming
Left Hand Pizzicato

Thumb Flex
Bow Lifts
Knee Benders
Sidewinder

$\frac{2}{4}$ Conducting Pattern

Finger Patterns on the G String

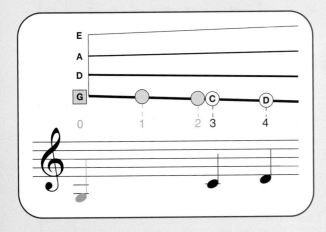

C = 3 Fingers Down

D = 4 Fingers Down

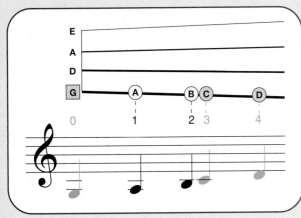

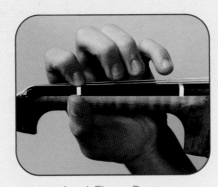

A = 1 Finger Down

B = 2 Fingers Down

74 Play D & C CD 1:74
Press the string firmly to the fingerboard.

75 Pumping Iron #5 CD 1:75

76 Pumping Iron #6 CD 1:76

77 Play B & A
Press the string firmly to the fingerboard.

78 Back and Forth on G CD 1:78

79 High Hurdles CD 1:79

80 Pole Vault CD 1:80

Creative Expression—Compose (Worksheet #17)

Orchestra @ Home

LESSON 1

1. Perform warm-ups to CD 1:73, "Brandenburg Concerto No. 5."

2. Practice "Lowdown Hoedown," concentrating on memorization. Play with the CD accompaniment and match your double-stops with the modeling.

3. Use pictures and descriptions on page 26 to prepare your fingers to play on the G string. Trim your fingernails to the proper length.

4. Play lines 74–76 pizzicato, shadow-bowing, and arco with their CD tracks.

LESSON 2

1. Review warm-ups to CD 1:73.

2. Practice lines 77–80 pizzicato, shadow-bowing, and arco with their CD tracks.

3. Review lines 74–78 shadow-bowing and arco with the CD tracks. Listen and match the melody line in the CD accompaniment. Concentrate on proper hand and arm position as you strive to play with a clear tone quality.

4. Complete your Creative Expression (Worksheet #17). Add the bowings. Complete the additional games.

LESSON 3

1. Perform warm-ups to CD 1:73.

2. Use pictures and descriptions on page 26 to prepare your fingers to play on the G string.

3. Play lines 74–80 with a clear tone quality to their CD tracks.

4. Show your family your composition and perform it for them. You may select one of the rhythm tracks (CD 1:13–16) as an accompaniment if you wish.

Warm-ups CD 1:73

Perfect Posture!
Orchestra Stretches #1 and #2
Finger Pattern Drill

Finger Pattern Sit-ups
Left Hand Strumming
Left Hand Pizzicato

Knee Benders
Sidewinder
Thumb Flex
Bow Lifts

$\frac{2}{4}$ Conducting Pattern

81 Pentascale #3 and Arpeggio CD 1:81
Start at the frog.

82 We Will Rock You!* CD 1:82
Words and Music by BRIAN MAY

This Arrangement © 2003 QUEEN MUSIC LTD.   All Rights Reserved

83 A Traveler's Song* CD 1:83
Change string levels with each pentascale.
Folk Song, Czech Republic

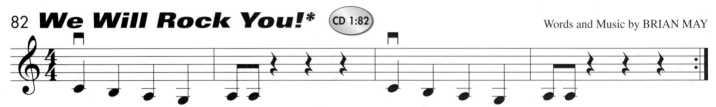

84 Ramadan Chant* CD 1:84
Use a fast bow stroke for eighth notes.
Folk Song, Kuwait

Orchestra @ Home

LESSON 1

1. Perform warm-ups to CD 1:73, "Brandenburg Concerto No. 5."
2. Practice lines 81–84 pizzicato, shadow-bowing, and arco with their CD accompaniments. Concentrate on keeping a steady tempo while using proper bow speed.
3. Play "We Will Rock You!" for your family.
4. Tell your family about the songs from the Czech Republic and Kuwait.
5. Create your composition using the creative tools listed on Worksheet #20. Complete the additional games.

LESSON 2

1. Perform warm-ups to CD 1:73.
2. Review lines 83–84. Play them for your family with the CD accompaniment.
3. Practice lines 85–86 pizzicato, shadow-bowing, and arco with their CD tracks.
4. Practice "Frogs' Legs" at a slower tempo, gradually increasing the speed.
5. Correct any errors in your composition, choose a tempo and a title, and practice it to perform for the class at our next meeting.

LESSON 3

1. Perform warm-ups to CD 1:73.
2. Review lines 82–87 with their CD tracks. Strive to play with a beautiful tone and correct intonation. Practice playing each song from memory.
3. Prepare to perform "The Traveler's Song" with good intonation. Strive to match the melody on the CD accompaniment.

Creative Tools of Music

Allegro—indicates a fast tempo

Andante—indicates a moderately slow walking tempo

Moderato—indicates a moderate tempo

Musical Style—a combination of all the elements of music resulting in the unique "flavor" of a culture or time period

Program Notes—written background material on pieces that are performed; usually included as part of the printed concert program

Tempo—indicates how fast or slow the music is to be played

Creative Expression—Compose (Worksheet #20)

85 Lightly Row* CD 1:85
Press the string firmly to the fingerboard.
Andante
Folk Song, Germany

86 Jingle Bells* CD 1:86
Allegro
JAMES PIERPONT, U.S.A.

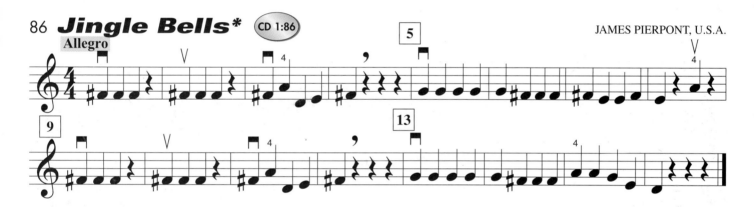

87 Frogs' Legs* CD 1:87
Use a fast bow stroke for the eighth notes.
Moderato
Folk Song, Hungary

Orchestra @ Home

LESSON 1

1. Perform warm-ups to CD 1:73, "Brandenburg Concerto No. 5."
2. Review lines 82–87 with their CD tracks. Strive to play in tune and with a good tone quality. Practice these melodies from memory.
3. Wash the soft cloth used to wipe the rosin dust from the instrument.

LESSON 2

1. Perform warm-ups to CD 1:73.
2. Review and practice all lines selected for the performance from memory.
3. Of the pieces not selected, choose your favorite and write a program note for it.

LESSON 3

1. Perform warm-ups to CD 1:73.
2. Perform a home concert of the selected lines using their CD tracks. Make sure you demonstrate proper concert procedures and concert etiquette.

Warm-ups CD 1:73

Perfect Posture!
Orchestra Stretches #1 and #2
Fingerboard Sliding
Fingerboard Tapping
Knee Benders
Sidewinder
Bow Taps
Thumb Flex
Bow Lifts
$\frac{2}{4}$ Conducting Pattern

Creative Tools of Music

Concerto—a multi-movement piece for orchestra that usually features one or more solo instruments

D Major Key Signature—indicates that all F's and C's are to be played sharp

Episode—sections of different material that alternate with the ritornello

Fortspinnung—a German word meaning the continuous "spinning forth" of new music

Key Signature—indicates what notes are to be played with sharps or flats

Ritornello—returning part; an Italian term referring to the opening musical material in a Baroque concerto played by the entire orchestra. This material keeps returning throughout the composition

Round—a melody in which different parts enter at staggered times but are exactly the same

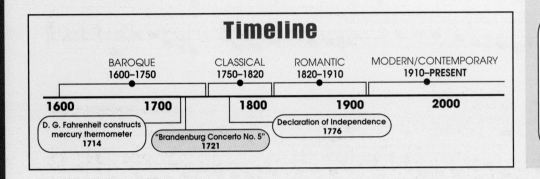

Timeline

	BAROQUE 1600–1750	CLASSICAL 1750–1820	ROMANTIC 1820–1910	MODERN/CONTEMPORARY 1910–PRESENT
	1600 ... 1700	1800	1900	2000

D. G. Fahrenheit constructs mercury thermometer 1714

"Brandenburg Concerto No. 5" 1721

Declaration of Independence 1776

Key of D Major

"Brandenburg Concerto No. 5" Listening Map

Ritornello (mm 1–8)   **Alternating Episodes and Ritornellos**

Ritornello Descriptor: _____

Conversation, Bridget Riley. Oil on linen.

PORTRAIT

Johann Sebastian Bach

J. S. Bach was a German composer who lived from 1685 to 1750. As a composer, he was considered a master of all baroque musical forms. He was employed by both the church and royalty at different times in his life. As well as being paid to compose, he was expected to play the organ at services, direct the choir and instrumentalists, and even teach grammar and Latin. He was married twice (his first wife died) and had 20 children, 10 of whom survived to adulthood. Many of his children became successful composers in the next generation of musicians.

88 Basses Play C♯   CD 1:88

Keep fingers down.

89 D Major Scale*   CD 1:89

Play with a full tone quality.

90 Johnny Works With One Hammer*   CD 1:90

Moderato

Folk Song, U.S.A.

91 The Clocks (Round)*   CD 1:91

Andante

Folk Song, Denmark

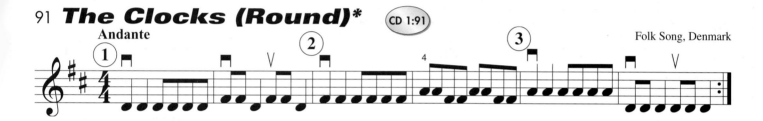

92 A la Brandenburg*   CD 1:92

Use a fast bow stroke for the eighth notes.

GERALD ANDERSON, U.S.A.

Allegro

Creative Expression—Improvise Movement to "Brandenburg Concerto No. 5"

Orchestra @ Home

LESSON 1

1. Review warm-ups to CD 1:73, "Brandenburg Concerto No. 5."

2. Practice "D Major Scale," carefully matching the pitches on its CD track.

3. Practice and begin memorizing "Johnny Works With One Hammer."

4. Tell your family about Bach and his dedication of the six concertos to the Margrave of Brandenburg.

LESSON 2

1. Review warm-ups to CD 1:73.

2. Practice lines 89–92 with their CD tracks. Think about the different bow speeds you will use for eighth notes and quarter notes. Begin memorizing these songs.

3. Play "The Clocks" as a round with friends.

4. Tell your family about J. S. Bach and how he supported his 20 children.

LESSON 3

1. Review warm-ups to CD 1:73.

2. Practice lines 89–92 with their CD tracks. Be aware of the varying bow speeds needed to keep a steady beat.

3. Continue to memorize these songs.

UNITS 16—18 WILL BE PRESENTED BY YOUR TEACHER

UNIT 19

Warm-ups 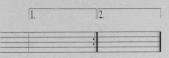 CD 2:3

Perfect Posture!
Orchestra Stretches #1 and #2
Fingerboard Sliding
Fingerboard Tapping
Knee Benders
Sidewinder
Bow Taps
Thumb Flex
Bow Lifts

Creative Tools of Music

♩ **Half Note**—two beats of sound, which is half the length of a whole note and twice the length of a quarter note

Half Rest—two beats of silence, which is half the length of a whole rest and twice the length of a quarter rest

1st and 2nd Endings—play the 1st ending the first time; repeat the same music, skip the 1st ending, and play the 2nd ending

---

Bow Division | **WB** = Whole Bow   **UH** = Upper Half   **LH** = Lower Half   **M** = Middle

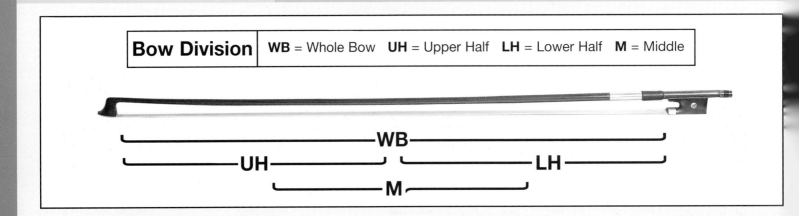

94 Half Full CD 2:4

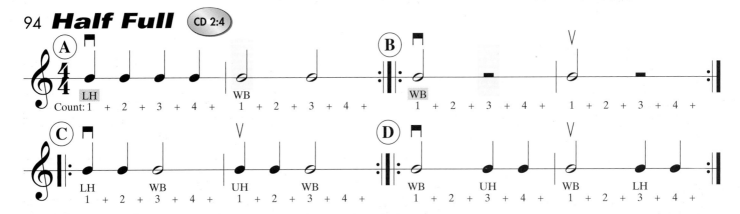

95 Descending D Major CD 2:5

Open and close your bow arm at the elbow.

96 Suo Gan* CD 2:6

Andante   Folk Song, Wales

97 **June, Lovely June* (Round)** CD 2:7

Folk Song, England

98 **Theme From New World Symphony*** CD 2:8

ANTONÌN DVORÀK, Czech Republic

Pull a smooth, straight bow.

99 **The Trolley Song*** CD 2:9

Music by RALPH BLANE
Lyrics by HUGH MARTIN

This Arrangement © 2003 METRO-GOLDWYN-MAYER INC. All Rights Reserved

100 **Creative Expression—**Improvise Over a Drone CD 2:10

101 **Kwanzaa*** CD 2:11

Swahili Folk Song, Africa

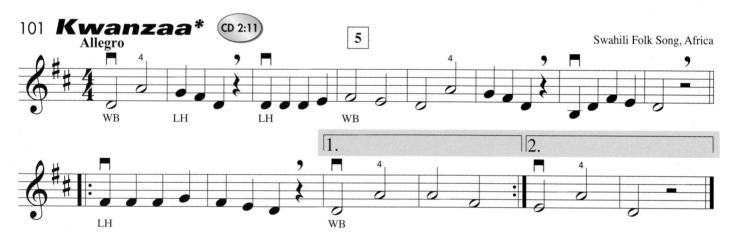

Orchestra @ Home

LESSON 1

1. Perform warm-ups to CD 2:3, "On the Beautiful Blue Danube."

2. Practice "Half Full" shadow-bowing and arco.

3. Practice "Descending D Major" using appropriate bow divisions.

4. Perform "Suo Gan" arco in a legato style.

LESSON 2

1. Perform the warm-ups to CD 2:3.

2. Review "Descending D Major" with its CD track. Play with good intonation.

3. Practice lines 96–98 slowly until you are able to play the string crossings smoothly. Begin to memorize these melodies.

LESSON 3

1. Perform warm-ups to CD 2:3.

2. Review songs 97–99. Prepare the bow division of "Theme From New World Symphony" for an assessment.

3. Practice "Kwanzaa" shadow-bowing and arco using its CD track.

LESSON 4

1. Perform warm-ups to CD 2:3.

2. Review the songs 97–101 concentrating on bow division with their CD tracks.

3. Practice "Kwanzaa" shadow-bowing and arco using it's CD track.

4. Improvise at home with notes D, E, and F♯ notes A, B, and C♯. Use half, quarter, and eighth notes.

Warm-ups

Perfect Posture!
Orchestra Stretches #1 and #2
Fingerboard Sliding
Fingerboard Tapping

Knee Benders
Sidewinder
Bow Taps
Thumb Flex
Bow Lifts

Creative Tools of Music

Slur—a curved line connecting two or more notes of different pitches played in the same bow stroke

Tie—a curved line connecting two notes of the same pitch and played as if they were one

102 *All Tied Up* (CD 2:12)

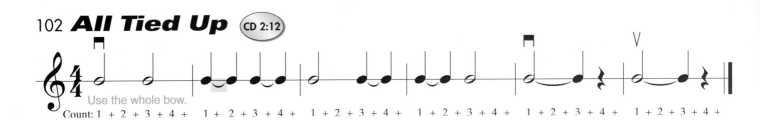

Use the whole bow.

Count: 1 + 2 + 3 + 4 + 1 + 2 + 3 + 4 + 1 + 2 + 3 + 4 + 1 + 2 + 3 + 4 + 1 + 2 + 3 + 4 + 1 + 2 + 3 + 4 +

103 **Smooth Slurs** (CD 2:13)

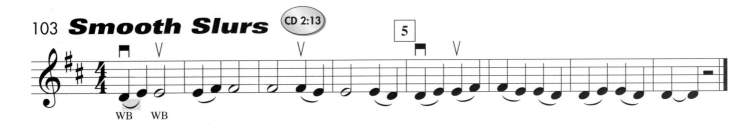

WB   WB

104 **Pentascales** (CD 2:14)

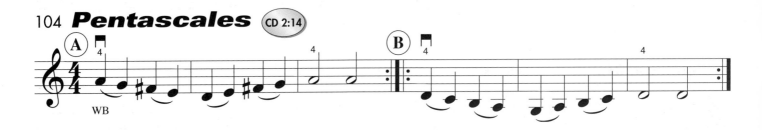

WB

105 *D Major Scale Slurred* (CD 2:15)

106 **String Crossings #1** (CD 2:16)

Keep fingers down on the D string, making a tunnel for open A.

107 **String Crossings #2** (CD 2:17)

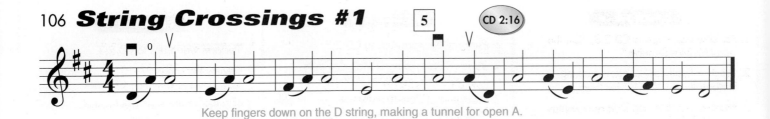

Keep fingers down on the D string.   Keep fingers down on the D string.

108 Theme From London Symphony* CD 2:18

Moderato

FRANZ JOSEPH HAYDN, Austria

1. 2.

109 Long, Long Ago* (Notation Expression) CD 2:19

Andante

THOMAS BAYLEY, England

Play very smoothly.

110 Over the Rainbow* CD 2:20

Andante

Music by HAROLD ARLEN
Lyric by E.Y. HARBURG

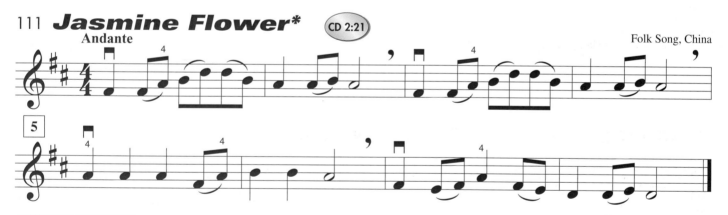

111 Jasmine Flower* CD 2:21

Andante

Folk Song, China

5

Orchestra @ Home

LESSON 1

1. Perform warm-ups to CD 2:3, "On the Beautiful Blue Danube."

2. Tell your family about ties and slurs. Perform lines 102–103 for them.

3. Practice your bow division as you play lines 102–105.

4. Select some favorite songs on pages 32–33. Perform them from memory with their CD Tracks.

LESSON 2

1. Perform warm-ups to CD 2:3.

2. Review lines 103–105. Concentrate on bow division. Prepare line 105 for an assessment of the bow division.

3. Practice lines 106–107. Try to cross the strings smoothly.

4. Tell your family about Franz Joseph Haydn (**Hi**-den) and the London Symphony.

5. Complete notating the bowings of "Long, Long Ago."

LESSON 3

1. Perform warm-ups to CD 2:3.

2. Review lines 105–108.

3. Prepare lines 106–107 for an assessment of smooth slurs and finger tunnels.

4. Practice lines 109–110. Strive to play smoothly with proper bow division.

LESSON 4

1. Perform warm-ups to CD 2:3.

2. Review lines 102–107. Concentrate on bow division and smooth slurring.

3. Practice lines 108–111. Match your pitches to the melodies on the CD.

UNIT 21

Warm-ups

Perfect Posture
Orchestra Stretches #1 and #2
Fingerboard Sliding
Fingerboard Tapping
Knee Benders
Sidewinder
Bow Taps
Thumb Flex
Bow Lifts

Creative Tools of Music

Anacrusis—one or more notes preceding the first complete measure

Dotted Half Note—receives three beats of sound in ¾ time; the dot after the note adds one half the value of the note

Duet—a composition with two different parts played simultaneously

Legato—play smoothly and connected

Time Signature—a time signature containing three beats in one measure with a quarter note receiving one beat

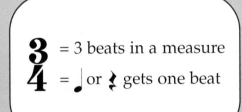

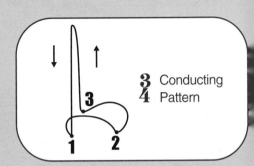

112 *Rhythms in 3* (CD 2:22)

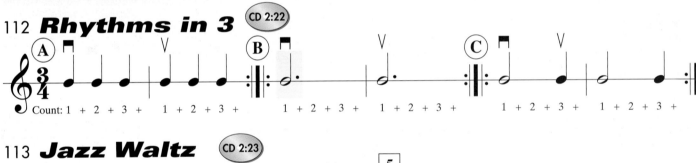

113 *Jazz Waltz* (CD 2:23)

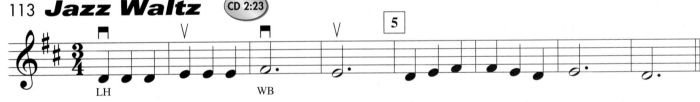

114 *Waltz in 3 D** (CD 2:24)

115 *French Folk Song** (CD 2:25)

Folk Song, France

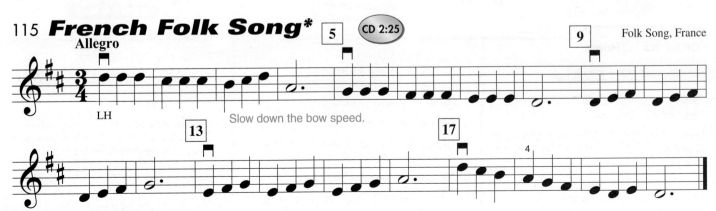

Slow down the bow speed.

Creative Expression—Improvise Over Chord Changes

116 Sweet Betsy From Pike* (Duet)

CD 2:26

Folk Song, U.S.A.

117 Look to the Rainbow*

CD 2:27

Words by E.Y. HARBURG
Music by BURTON LANE

118 Lullaby*

CD 2:28

JOHANNES BRAHMS, Germany

Orchestra @ Home

LESSON 1

1. Perform warm-ups to CD 2:3, "On the Beautiful Blue Danube."

2. Demonstrate the 3/4 conducting pattern to your family snd conduct "On the Beautiful Blue Danube" with the CD track.

3. Practice lines 112–115. Concentrate on bow division and bow speed.

4. Review lines 109–111. Strive to play smoothly and with proper bow division.

LESSON 2

1. Perform warm-ups to CD 2:3.

2. Review lines 112–115 with a legato style.

3. Prepare line 113 for assessment of bow division/speed and a legato style.

4. Practice both parts of line 116.

5. Practice line 117. Play with proper bow division/speed and in a legato style.

LESSONS 3 & 4

1. Perform warm-ups to CD 2:3.

2. Review lines 113–118 playing with a legato bowing style. Be sure to play both lines of the duet with the CD track.

3. Perform the melodies for your family from memory.

4. Practice improvising on the D and A strings with CD 2:10. Play four-measures each of D string notes, A string notes, and D string notes.

37

Warm-ups

Perfect Posture!

Orchestra Stretches #1 and #2

Finger Pattern Sit-ups

Finger Twister Games

Fingerboard Sliding

Fingerboard Tapping

Knee Benders

Sidewinder

Bow Taps

Thumb Flex

Bow Lifts

¾ Conducting Pattern

*Study for a Tapestry
(study for Spatial Ikat III)*, 1976.
Lia Cook (b. 1943).

Serigraph on paper, 9 1/4 x 15 11/16 in.
(23.4 x 39.9 cm.). © Lia Cook. Transparency:
© Smithsonian American Art Museum,
Washington, DC/Art Resource, NY.

Creative Tools of Music

Slurred Staccato (hooked bowing)—two or more notes played in the same direction with a stop between each note

Staccato—notes marked with a dot above or below the note head; stop the bow between notes

Waltz—a popular dance for couples in ¾ time

PORTRAIT

Johann Strauss II

The Strauss family of Vienna, Austria were well known as musicians. Johann Strauss Sr. was both a composer and conductor. He wanted Johann Strauss II to be a banker; instead, the younger Strauss secretly studied the violin and composed numerous pieces until his debut at the age of 19. Johann Strauss II became well known for his beautiful melodies and his ability to compose quickly. It has been said he would begin a composition in the morning, members of the orchestra would copy the parts and rehearse it that afternoon, and Strauss would conduct the new waltz that night. In Vienna, a city where everyone loved to dance, the waltz was the music of choice, and Johann Strauss II became known as the Waltz King of "On the Beautiful Blue Danube" stands as a masterwork of the waltz style.

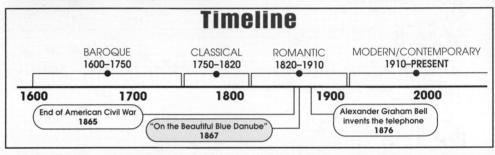

"On the Beautiful Blue Danube" Listening Map

Waltz 1	Waltz 2	Waltz 3
A:‖:B:‖	A‖B‖A	‖:A:‖B‖

119 ***Taco Staccato*** CD 2:29

120 ***Staccato March**** CD 2:30
Moderato
GERALD ANDERSON, U.S.A.

Stop the bow on notes marked staccato.

Creative Expression—Improvise Movement in 3/4 Time

121 Learn Slurred Staccato   CD 2:31

Keep the bow on the string. Do not lift.

122 Hooked on 4/4   CD 2:32

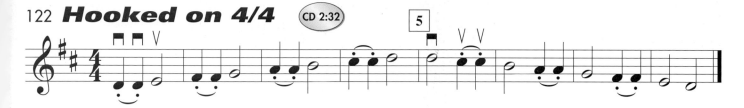

123 Hooked on 3/4   CD 2:33

124 On the Beautiful Blue Danube*   CD 2:34
(Orchestra Arrangement)

JOHANN STRAUSS, II, Austria
Arranged by SANDRA DACKOW, U.S.A.

Moderato

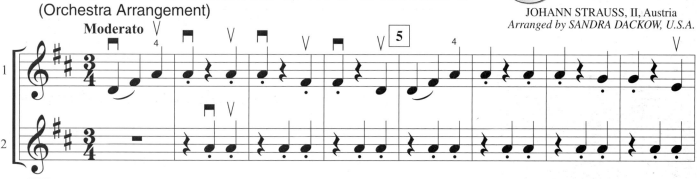

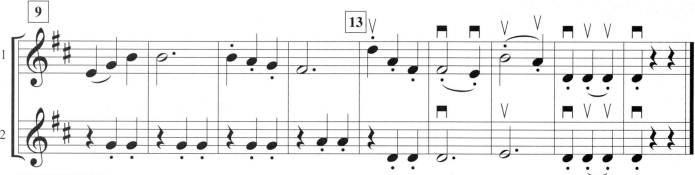

Orchestra @ Home

LESSON 1

1. Perform warm-ups to CD 2:3, "On the Beautiful Blue Danube."

2. Practice lines 119–123 with their CD tracks. Begin each staccato bow with a pinch of the forefinger on the bow. Keep your bow stroke short and crisp.

3. Perform "Staccato March" for your family with its CD accompaniment.

4. Tell your family about Johann Strauss II and his waltz "On the Beautiful Blue Danube."

LESSON 2

1. Perform warm-ups to CD 2:3.

2. Practice lines 119–124 with their CD tracks using good staccato technique.

3. Prepare "Staccato March" for assessment, concentrating on staccato and legato bowings and perform it for your family.

LESSON 3

1. Perform warm-ups to CD 2:3.

2. Practice lines 119–124 with their CD tracks using good staccato technique.

3. Perform "On The Beautiful Blue Danube" for your family with its CD accompaniment.

4. Tell your family about the form of "On the Beautiful Blue Danube."

UNIT 23

Warm-ups CD 2:35

Perfect Posture!
Orchestra Stretches #1 and #2
Finger Pattern Drill
Finger Pattern Sit-ups
Fingerboard Sliding
Fingerboard Tapping
Kneebenders
Sidewinder
Bow Taps
Thumb Flex
Bow Lifts

Creative Tools of Music

Chromatics—notes altered with sharps, flats, or naturals

Half Step—the smallest distance between two notes

Interval—the distance between two pitches

Natural—a sign that cancels a sharp or flat

Whole Step—a step made of two half steps

New Finger Pattern on the D String

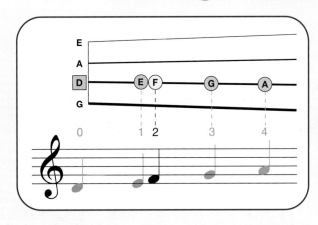

F♮ = 2 Fingers Down

126 Learn F♮ CD 2:36

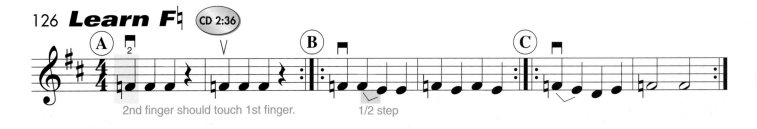

2nd finger should touch 1st finger.   1/2 step

127 Watch Your Step! CD 2:37

whole step

128 Chromatic Calisthenics #1 CD 2:38

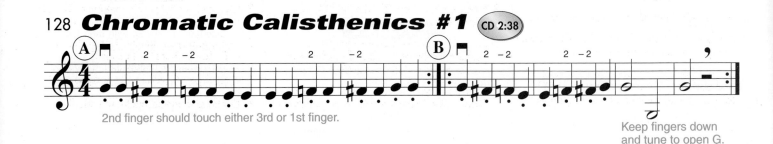

2nd finger should touch either 3rd or 1st finger.

Keep fingers down
and tune to open G.

40

129 Bass Shifter CD 2:39

130 Pentascale #4 and Arpeggio CD 2:40

131 Hotaru Koi* CD 2:41

Andante

Folk Song, Japan

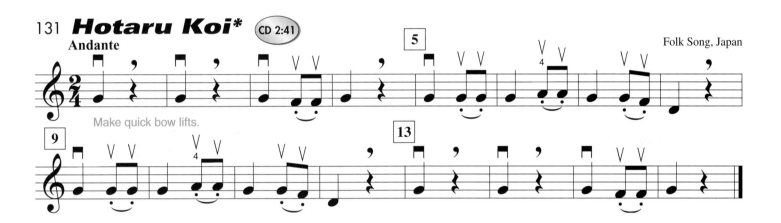

Make quick bow lifts.

132 Low 2 Blues* CD 2:42

Moderato

Music by ROBERT W. SMITH, U.S.A.
Words by SANDRA DACKOW, U.S.A.

Orchestra @ Home

LESSON 1

1. Perform warm-ups to CD 2:35, "Danse Infernale."

2. Trim your fingernails to the proper length.

3. Practice lines 126–130 with their CD tracks. Watch your second finger placement.

4. Explain how chromatics affect the notes and perform "Chromatic Calisthenics #1" for your family with its CD accompaniment.

LESSON 2

1. Perform warm-ups to CD 2:35.

2. Practice lines 126–132 with their CD tracks. Watch your second finger placement.

3. Prepare "Chromatic Calisthenics #1" to perform for the class. Carefully match your pitches to the melody on the CD.

4. Perform for your family "Hotaru Koi" and "Low 2 Blues" with their CD accompaniments.

LESSON 3

1. Perform warm-ups to CD 2:35.

2. Practice lines 126–132 with their CD tracks. Watch your second finger placement.

3. Perform for your family "Hotaru Koi" and "Low 2 Blues" with their CD accompaniments. Tell them how bowing techniques affect the style of the music.

4. Continue to memorize these melodies.

UNIT 24

Perfect Posture!   Finger Twister Games   Knee Benders   Thumb Flex
Orchestra Stretches #1 and #2   Fingerboard Sliding   Sidewinder   Bow Lifts
Finger Pattern Sit-ups   Fingerboard Tapping   Bow Taps

New Finger Pattern on the A String

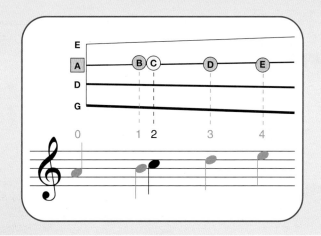

C♮ = 2 Fingers Down

133 **Learn C♮**   CD 2:43

2nd finger should touch 1st finger.

134 **Steppin' Out**   CD 2:44

135 **Chromatic Calisthenics #2**   CD 2:45

2nd finger should touch either 3rd or 1st finger.

Keep fingers down
and tune to open D.

136 **Shifty Business**   CD 2:46

137 **Pentascale #5 and Arpeggio**   CD 2:47

Creative Expression—Compose (Worksheet #35)

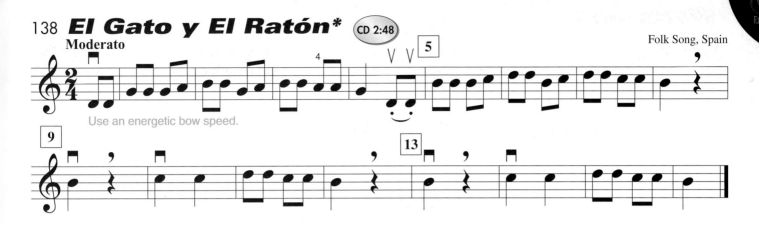

138 *El Gato y El Ratón** CD 2:48
Moderato
Folk Song, Spain
Use an energetic bow speed.

139 **The Snake Charmer** CD 2:49
Andante
Folk Song, France
Play legato.

140 **Wipe Out** CD 2:50
Moderato
By THE SURFARIS
Slide 2nd finger quickly on the string.

This Arrangement © 2003 MIRALESTE MUSIC and ROBIN HOOD MUSIC CO.   All Rights Reserved   Used by Permission

Orchestra @ Home

LESSON 1

1. Perform warm-ups to CD 2:35, "Danse Infernale."
2. Trim your fingernails to the proper length.
3. Practice lines 133–137 with their CD tracks. Watch your second finger placement.
4. Perform for your family "Chromatic Calisthenics #2" with its CD accompaniment.

LESSON 2

1. Perform warm-ups to CD 2:35.
2. Practice lines 133–139 with their CD tracks. Watch your second finger placement.

3. Perform for your family "El Gato y El Ratón" and "The Snake Charmer" with their CD accompaniments.

LESSON 3

1. Perform warm-ups to CD 2:35.
2. Practice lines 133–140 with their CD tracks.
3. Prepare line 135 for assessment at our next class. Concentrate on the chromatic finger patterns and playing with good intonation.
4. Perform for your family "El Gato y El Ratón," "The Snake Charmer," and "Wipe Out" with their CD accompaniments.
5. Complete your composition.

LESSON 4

1. Perform warm-ups to CD 2:35.
2. Practice lines 135–140 with their CD tracks.
3. Edit your composition. Give it a name and a tempo marking. Practice it to perform for the class. Perform it for your family.

LESSON 5

1. Perform warm-ups to CD 2:35.
2. Practice lines 135–140 with their CD tracks.
3. Perform your favorite "low 2" songs for your family. Play from memory if you can.

UNIT 25

Warm-ups CD 2:35

Perfect Posture!   Finger Pattern Sit-ups   Knee Benders   Thumb Flex

Orchestra Stretches #1 and #2   Fingerboard Sliding   Sidewinder   Bow Lifts

Finger Pattern Drill   Fingerboard Tapping   Bow Taps

141 **Learn 4th Position on the G String (Cello)**

142 **Matching Pitches on the D and G Strings** **(Cello)**

143 **Learn 4th Position on the D String (Cello)**

144 **Matching Pitches on the A and D Strings** **(Cello)**

Igor Stravinsky

Igor Stravinsky was a Russian composer, who lived from 1882 to 1971. During the Russian Revolution of 1917, he moved to France for political reasons. In 1940, he moved to the U.S., where he spent the remainder of his life. His first composition to achieve international acclaim was *The Firebird,* which he completed in 1910. This ballet helped usher in a new 20th-century style that challenged listeners and performers in many ways. Stravinsky's works featured complex harmonies, irregular rhythms and time signatures, and melodies with unpredictable leaps. He pushed instruments into extended ranges and required that players learn difficult new techniques. His music often sounded brutal or primitive. Stravinsky also featured many folk songs and dances in his music and borrowed famous themes from other composers to use in his own compositions. He was a driving force behind most of the important musical developments of the first half of the 20th-century.

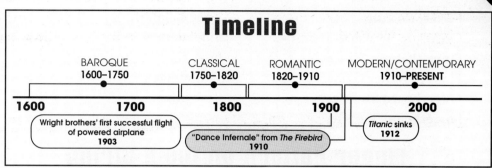

Timeline

BAROQUE 1600–1750	CLASSICAL 1750–1820	ROMANTIC 1820–1910	MODERN/CONTEMPORARY 1910–PRESENT
1600	1700	1800	1900	2000

Wright brothers' first successful flight of powered airplane 1903

"Dance Infernale" from *The Firebird* 1910

Titanic sinks 1912

"Danse Infernale" Listening Map

Section 1	Section 2	Section 3	Section 4
Exposition Theme A	Development of Theme A Introduce Theme B	Further development of Theme A	Coda (ending) I Theme C+
		Transition (getting faster)	All 3 themes compressed

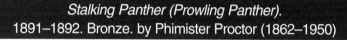

Stalking Panther (Prowling Panther).
1891–1892. Bronze. by Phimister Proctor (1862–1950)

145 *Danse Infernale** CD 2:55

Allegro

By IGOR STRAVINSKY, Russia, France, U.S.A.

LH

5

Creative Expression—Create Movement to "Danse Infernale"

Orchestra @ Home

LESSON 1

1. Perform warm-ups to CD 2:35, "Danse Infernale."

2. Practice lines 141–144 with their CD tracks.

3. Tell your family about "Danse Infernale" from *The Firebird.*

LESSON 2

1. Perform warm-ups to CD 2:35.

2. Practice lines 141–145 with their CD tracks.

3. Tell your family about Igor Stravinsky and 20th-century music.

4. Play some of your favorite songs from memory.

LESSON 3

1. Perform warm-ups to CD 2:35.

2. Practice lines 141–145 with their CD tracks.

3. Tell your family about the form of "Danse Infernale" music.

4. Play for your family "Danse Infernale" with its CD track.

Warm-ups (CD 2:56)

Perfect Posture!
Orchestra Stretches #1 and #2
Finger Pattern Sit-ups
Finger Twister Games
Fingerboard Sliding
Fingerboard Tapping

Knee Benders
Sidewinder
Bow Taps
Thumb Flex
Bow Lifts

Creative Tools of Music

G Major Key Signature—indicates that all F's are to be played as F♯

Octave—the interval from one note to the next note of the same name, up or down

Finger Pattern on the E String

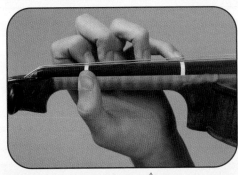

F♯, G, A, B = 1̂2 3 4

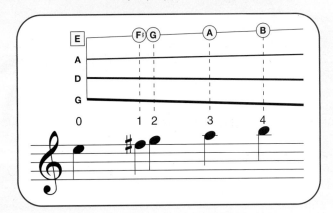

Key of G Major

147 Learn the Open E String (Violins and Basses) (CD 2:57)

Adjust the arm height for each string level.

148 Learn B and A (Violins and Basses) (CD 2:58)

149 Pumping Iron #7 (CD 2:59)

150 Learn G and F♯ (Violins and Basses) (CD 2:60)

151 **Half Step Dash** CD 2:61

2nd finger should touch 1st finger.

152 **Long Jump** CD 2:62

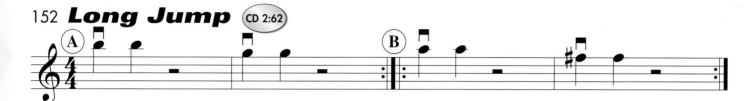

153 **Low Hurdles** CD 2:63

154 **Pentascale #6 and Arpeggio** CD 2:64

155 **G Major Scale #1 and Arpeggio*** CD 2:65

156 **G Major Scale #2 and Arpeggio*** CD 2:66

 **Creative Expression—**Compose (Worksheet #39)

Orchestra @ Home

LESSON 1

1. Perform warm-ups to CD 2:56, "Spring."

2. Trim your fingernails to the proper length.

3. Practice lines 147–154 with their CD tracks. Watch your second finger placement.

4. Perform for your family "Pentascale #6 and Arpeggio" with its CD accompaniment. Strive for good intonation, matching the string modeling.

5. Remove all rosin dust from the instrument body and strings with a soft cloth.

LESSON 2

1. Perform warm-ups to CD 2:56.

2. Practice lines 147–156 with their CD tracks. Watch your second finger placement.

3. Finish your eight-measure composition (Worksheet #39) and perform it for your family. Tell them about the title and the style of your music. Complete the additional games.

4. Remove all rosin dust from the instrument and strings with a soft cloth. Carefully pack the instrument away.

LESSON 3

1. Perform warm-ups to CD 2:56.

2. Practice lines 149 and 151–156 with their CD tracks. Watch your second finger placement.

3. Re-evaluate and edit your composition. Practice it with Rhythm Tracks 13–16 on CD 1 and select one that best fits the style of your music.

Warm-ups CD 2:71

Perfect Posture!   Finger Pattern Sit-ups   Knee Benders   Thumb Flex
Orchestra Stretches #1 and #2 Fingerboard Sliding   Sidewinder   Bow Lifts
Finger Pattern Drill   Fingerboard Tapping   Bow Taps

157 **El Charro*** CD 2:67
Allegro
Folk Song, Mexico
Slow Fast Slow Fast Fast Slow
bow. bow. bow. bow. bow. bow.

158 **El Tren*** CD 2:68
Allegro
Folk Song, Venezuela
Adjust arm height for string levels.

159 **Perica*** CD 2:69
Moderato
Folk Song, Chile
Slow Fast
bow. bow.

160A **Happy Birthday to You!*** CD 2:70
Moderato
Words and Music by
MILDRED J. HILL and PATTY S. HILL

This Arrangement © 2003 SUMMY-BIRCHARD MUSIC, a division of SUMMY-BIRCHARD INC.   All Rights Reserved

160B **Feliz Cumpleaños*** CD 2:70
Allegro
Words and Music by
MILDRED J. HILL and PATTY S. HILL
Arranged by VICTOR LOPEZ

This Arrangement © 2003 SUMMY-BIRCHARD MUSIC, a division of SUMMY-BIRCHARD INC.   All Rights Reserved

Creative Expression—Improvise to Latin-American Rhythms

48

Creative Tools of Music

Concerto—a multi-movement piece for orchestra that features one or more solo instruments

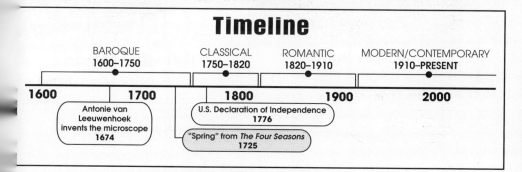

Timeline

BAROQUE 1600–1750	CLASSICAL 1750–1820	ROMANTIC 1820–1910	MODERN/CONTEMPORARY 1910–PRESENT

1600   1700   1800   1900   2000

- Antonie van Leeuwenhoek invents the microscope 1674
- U.S. Declaration of Independence 1776
- "Spring" from *The Four Seasons* 1725

"Spring" Listening Map

A Section	**B** Section	**C** Section	**D** Section	**E** Section	Closing
Spring...	*Festively...*	*And with the...*	*Lightning...*	*Once they...*	
Ritornello	3 Violins	Slurred Notes	16th Notes	3 Violins	Ritornello

PORTRAIT

Antonio Vivaldi

Antonio Vivaldi was an Italian composer who lived from 1678 to 1741. He was ordained as a priest in 1703. Because of his flaming red hair, he was nicknamed "The Red Priest." Also in 1703 he became the violin instructor at the Venetian Ospedale (Venice Orphanage-Conservatory), a position he held off and on for most of his career. His reputation as a composer and violin virtuoso spread rapidly. It attracted daughters of the nobility to seek places in the music program originally designed for orphaned girls. Vivaldi is celebrated for his superb craftsmanship and enormous output of more than 500 concertos.

Mochibana (Rice Cake and Flowers) by Keiko Kodai. 17 x 12 ½ in.

© 2002 The Wing Gallery

161 **Spring** (Orchestra Arrangement)   CD 2:71

ANTONIO VIVALDI, Italy
Arranged by SANDRA DACKOW, U.S.A.

Orchestra @ Home — Your teacher will give you the lesson assignments.

UNIT 29

Warm-ups CD 2:72

Perfect Posture!
Orchestra Stretches #1 and #2
Finger Pattern Sit-ups
Finger Twister Games
Fingerboard Sliding
Fingerboard Tapping
Knee Benders
Sidewinder
Bow Taps
Thumb Flex
Bow Lifts

Creative Tools of Music

C Major Key Signature—indicates that all notes are to be played as naturals

Ostinato—a repeated melodic or rhythmic pattern

Key of C Major

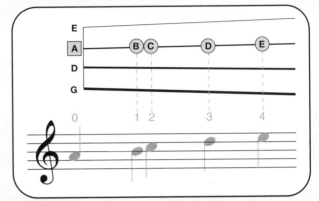

Review Finger Patterns

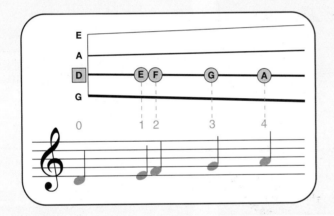

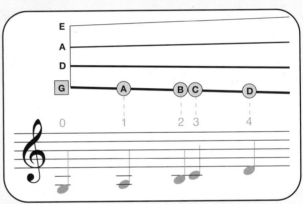

163 Learn the Open C String (Violas and Cellos) CD 2:73

Adjust the arm height for each string level.

164 Learn G and F (Violas and Cellos) CD 2:74

165 Pumping Iron #8 CD 2:75

166 Learn E and D (Violas and Cellos) CD 2:76

167 **Whole Step Dash** CD 2:77

168 **Pentascale #7 and Arpeggio** CD 2:78

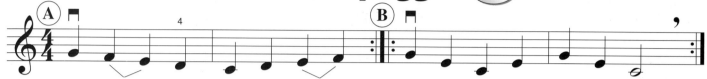

169 **Learn II Position (Basses)** CD 2:79

170 **C Major Scale #1 and Arpeggio*** CD 2:80

171 **C Major Scale #2 and Arpeggio*** CD 2:81

172 **Theme From Symphony No. 1*** CD 2:82

JOHANNES BRAHMS, Germany

Creative Expression—Improvise Over a Rhythmic Ostinato

Orchestra @ Home

LESSON 1

1. Perform warm-ups to CD 2:72, "Academic Festival Overture."

2. Practice lines 163–169 with their CD tracks. Watch your second finger placement.

3. Perform for your family "Pentascale #7 and Arpeggio" with its CD accompaniment.

4. Improvise rhythmic patterns on the open D string using CD 1 Rhythm Tracks 13–16.

LESSON 2

1. Perform warm-ups to CD 2:72.

2. Practice lines 163–171 with their CD tracks. Watch your second finger placement.

3. Match your pitches to the melodies on the CD tracks.

4. Practice line 172, setting the bow at the midpoint to begin with the anacrusis. Strive to play with a legato style.

LESSON 3

1. Perform warm-ups to CD 2:72.

2. Practice lines 165–172 with their CD tracks. Watch your second finger placement.

3. Perform for your family "Theme from Symphony No. 1" with its CD accompaniment.

Warm-ups (CD 2:72)

Perfect Posture!
Orchestra Stretches #1 and #2
Fingerboard Tapping
Fingerboard Sliding
Knee Benders
Sidewinder
Bow Taps
Thumb Flex
Bow Lifts

Creative Tools of Music

C Common Time Signature— the same as a 4/4 time signature

o Whole Note—a note twice as long as a half note

━ Whole Rest—a rest twice as long as a half rest

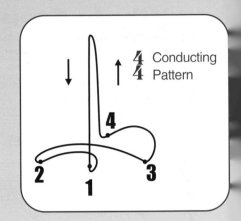

4/4 Conducting Pattern

Johannes Brahms

Johannes Brahms' first music teacher was his father, a string bass player in the Philharmonic Society in Hamburg, Germany. From a young age, Brahms studied piano and made his first public appearance at the age of ten. Soon after, Brahms began to earn a little money by playing piano in taverns and restaurants. He continued his studies and performances and, at the age 20, was introduced to the famous composer Robert Schumann. Of that meeting Schumann noted in his journal, "Johannes Brahms, a genius." Brahms never departed from his humble roots; he preferred to dine in simple restaurants and wear a loose-fitting flannel shirt instead of formal clothes. Even so, Brahms' music was admired by patrons of the arts across the world and from all social levels. Although he held various posts as an artistic director, he followed Beethoven's example as one of the new breed of composers/entrepreneurs who earned most of their income through commissions/contracts for their music.

Academic Festival Overture

In 1879 Breslau University awarded Johannes Brahms the honorary degree of Doctor of Philosophy. Brahms wrote Academic Festival Overture in return for this honor. It is based on student songs that were popular at the time. The popular student song "Gaudeamus Igitur" is the theme in our Masterwork. The text of the song is about living life to its fullest while one is young.

Timeline

BAROQUE 1600–1750	CLASSICAL 1750–1820	ROMANTIC 1820–1910	MODERN/CONTEMPORARY 1910–PRESENT

1600	1700	1800	1900	2000

Alexander Graham Bell invents the telephone 1876

Symphony No. 1 1876

"Academic Festival Overture" 1881

Sir Charles Parsons invents the first practical steam turbine engine 1884

"Academic Festival Overture" Listening Map

Transition	Song 1	Transition	Song 2	Transition to 2/4	Song 3	Song 4 in 3/4
transition	Vln,Ww,Br	Vlns,Ww	Vln / Ww	Strgs / Ww	Br / Ww	Br / Ww
C Major	C Major	G Major	C Major	Bb Major to C	C Major	C Major

Thematic Descriptors: _____ _____ _____ _____

United States Naval Academy Graduation Hat-Toss

Photograph Courtesy of the United States Naval Academy Photography Lab, Annapolis, Maryland.

173 Sakura* CD 2:83

Andante · Folk Song, Japan

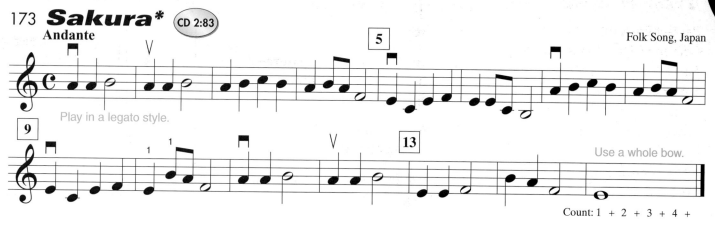

Play in a legato style.

Use a whole bow.

Count: 1 + 2 + 3 + 4 +

174 Kookaburra* CD 2:84

By MARION SINCLAIR

Moderato

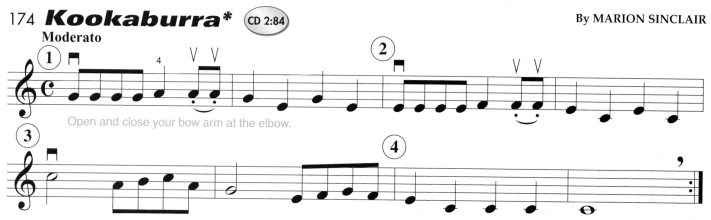

Open and close your bow arm at the elbow.

© 1932 Larrikin Music c/o Music Sales Corp. All Rights Reserved. Used by Permission.

175 Gaudeamus Igitur* CD 2:85
(Orchestra Arrangement)

JOHANNES BRAHMS, Germany
Arranged by SANDRA DACKOW, U.S.A.

Andante

Creative Expression—Compose (Worksheet #43)

Orchestra @ Home —Your teacher will give you the lesson assignments.

Warm-ups

Perfect Posture!
Orchestra Stretches #1 and #2
Finger Pattern Drill
Finger Pattern Sit-ups
Left Hand Strumming
Left Hand Pizzicato
Fingerboard Sliding
Fingerboard Tapping

Knee Benders
Sidewinder
Bow Taps
Thumb Flex
Bow Lifts

Creative Tools of Music

Da Capo al Fine—return to the beginning and play to the fine (end), usually not including the repeats

Divisi (div.)—the part is divided; two parts are written on one staff and are played by different performers

Unison (unis.)—all play the same notes and rhythms

176 **Do Ra Ji*** CD 2:86 — Folk Song, Korea
Andante — Repeat!

177 **El Florón*** CD 2:87 — Folk Song, Puerto Rico
Allegro

178 **Robo Rock*** CD 2:88 — VICTOR LOPEZ, U.S.A.
(Orchestra Arrangement)
Allegro

179 Bling! Blang!* CD 2:89

Words and Music by WOODY GUTHRIE

Use a fast bow stroke on the eighth notes.

This Arrangement © 2003 Folkways Music Publishers, Inc.   All Rights Reserved   Used by Permission

180 Music for the Royal Fireworks* CD 2:90 CD 2:91

(Orchestra Arrangement)

GEORGE F. HÄNDEL, Germany and England
Arranged by SANDRA DACKOW, U.S.A.

Orchestra @ Home

LESSON 1

1. Perform warm-ups to a masterwork of your choice.

2. Review lines 170–171. Concentrate on finger patterns and good intonation.

3. Tell your family about the Latin-American origin of "El Florón." Perform it for them. Be aware of the bow division/speeds needed to perform this song correctly.

LESSON 2

1. Perform warm-ups to a masterwork of your choice.

2. Review lines 170–171. Concentrate on finger patterns and good intonation.

3. Apply your knowledge of the C major scale to "Gaudeamus Igitur." Practice both the melody and orchestra lines.

4. Review "El Florón," concentrating on a beautiful legato style.

5. Practice "Robo Rock." Violins and violas should practice both melody and orchestra parts.

LESSON 3 & 4

1. Perform warm-ups to a masterwork of your choice.

2. Practice "Robo Rock." Violins and violas should practice both melody and orchestra parts and match the rock bowing style.

3. Review line 89 on page 30. Concentrate on finger patterns and good intonation.

4. Review "Bling-Blang" concentrating on finger patterns, bow division, and bow speed.

5. Tell your family about George Frideric Handel and "Music for the Royal Fireworks." Perform both melody and orchestra parts with the CD accompaniment.

UNITS 34-36
ARE PRESENTED BY YOUR TEACHER

Glossary

Page numbers refer to the Student Book page where the definition is shown.

1st and 2nd Ending—*Play the 1st ending the first time; repeat the same music, skip the 1st ending, and play the 2nd ending (32)*

ABA form—*A musical form consisting of three sections in which the third section is the same as the first; same, different, same (8)*

Allegro—*Indicates a fast tempo (29)*

Anacrusis—*One or more notes preceding the first complete measure (36)*

Andante—*Indicates a moderately slow walking tempo (29)*

Arco—*Play with the bow (10)*

Arpeggio—*Notes of a chord played one at a time (22)*

Balance Point of the Bow—*The point where the stick remains totally horizontal when balanced on the forefinger (24)*

Ballet—*A story told through music and dance (24)*

Bar Line—*The vertical line that divides the music staff into measures (8)*

Bow Lift—*Raise the bow from the string and return it to the original starting point (17)*

Bridge—*A transitional musical passage connecting two themes or sections (24)*

Chord—*Three or more notes sounded at the same time (22)*

Chromatics—*Notes altered with sharps, flats, or naturals (40)*

Clef Sign—*A symbol placed at the beginning of the staff used to identify the lines and spaces (8)*

Coda—*A short ending section of music (24)*

C Common Time Signature—*The same as a ⁴₄ time signature (52)*

Concerto—*A multi-movement piece for orchestra that usually features one or more solo instruments (30, 49)*

Da Capo al Fine—*Return to the beginning and play to the Fine (end), usually not including the repeats (54)*

Divisi (div.)—*The part is divided; two parts are written on one staff and are played by different performers (54)*

Dotted Half Note—*Receives three beats of sound in ³₄ time; the dot after the note adds one half the value of the note (36)*

Double Bar—*Two vertical lines placed on the staff to indicate the end of a section or composition (14)*

Double Stop—*Two notes played at the same time (24)*

Down bow—*Pull the bow toward the tip (10)*

Duet—*A composition with two different parts played simultaneously (36)*

Eighth Note—*A note one half the value of a quarter note (24)*

Episode—*Sections of different material that alternate with the Ritornello (30)*

Fine—*The end (54)*

Fortspinnung—*A German word meaning the continuous "spinning forth" of new music (30)*

Half note—*A note half the length of a whole note and twice the length of a quarter note (32)*

Half rest—*A rest half the length of a whole rest and twice the length of a quarter rest (32)*

Half Step—*The smallest distance between two notes (40)*

Hoo-Hoo—*A cardboard/PVC pipe tube used to shadow bow (10)*

Improvisation—*The spontaneous creation of music within specified guidelines (5)*

Interval—*The distance between two pitches (40)*

Intonation—*How well each note is played in tune (12)*

Introduction—*A short section of music at the beginning of a composition (24)*

Key Signature—*Indicates what notes are to be played with sharps or flats (30, 46, 50)*

Ledger lines—*Short lines to extend the range of the staff higher or lower (10)*

Legato—*Play smoothly and connected (36)*

March—*Rhythmic music for the uniform movement of groups of people (8)*

Measure—*The space between two bar lines to form a grouping of beats (8)*

Moderato—*Indicates a moderate tempo (29)*